Trail of Tears

An Enthralling Guide to the Choctaw and Chickasaw Removal, the Seminole Wars, Creek Dissolution, and Forced Relocation of the Cherokee Tribe

© Copyright 2022 - All rights reserved.

The content contained within this book may not be reproduced, duplicated, or transmitted without direct written permission from the author or the publisher.

Under no circumstances will any blame or legal responsibility be held against the publisher, or author, for any damages, reparation, or monetary loss due to the information contained within this book, either directly or indirectly.

Legal Notice:

This book is copyright protected. It is only for personal use. You cannot amend, distribute, sell, use, quote, or paraphrase any part, or the content within this book, without the consent of the author or publisher.

Disclaimer Notice:

Please note the information contained within this document is for educational and entertainment purposes only. All effort has been executed to present accurate, up-to-date, reliable, and complete information. No warranties of any kind are declared or implied. Readers acknowledge that the author is not engaging in the rendering of legal, financial, medical, or professional advice. The content within this book has been derived from various sources. Please consult a licensed professional before attempting any techniques outlined in this book.

By reading this document, the reader agrees that under no circumstances is the author responsible for any losses, direct or indirect, that are incurred as a result of the use of the information contained within this document, including, but not limited to, errors, omissions, or inaccuracies.

Free limited time bonus

Stop for a moment. We have a free bonus set up for you. The problem is this: we forget 90% of everything that we read after 7 days. Crazy fact, right? Here's the solution: we've created a printable, 1-page pdf summary for this book that you're reading now. All you have to do to get your free pdf summary is to go to the following website: **https://livetolearn.lpages.co/enthrallinghistory/**

Once you do, it will be intuitive. Enjoy, and thank you!

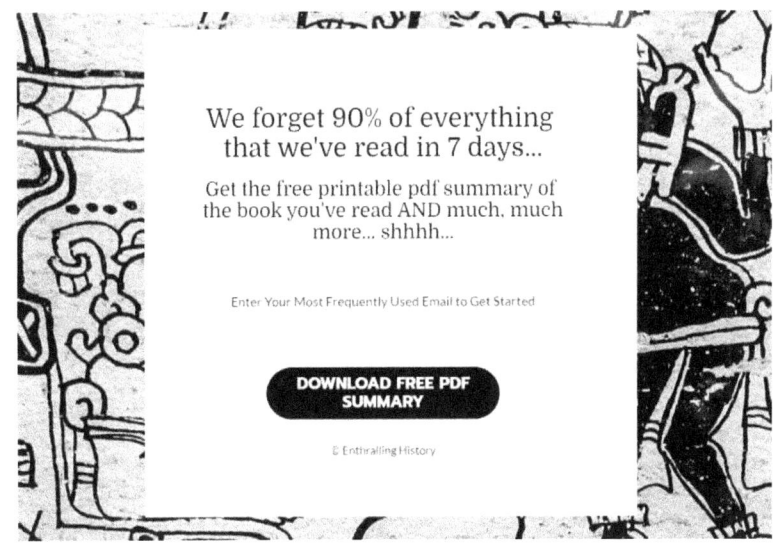

Table of Contents

INTRODUCTION 1
CHAPTER 1: THE FIVE CIVILIZED TRIBES 2
CHAPTER 2: SINISTER ORIGINS 10
CHAPTER 3: THE INDIAN REMOVAL ACT 1830: CAUSE AND CONSEQUENCE 17
CHAPTER 4: SEMINOLE RESISTANCE: THIS MEANS WAR 24
CHAPTER 5: MANIFEST DESTINY: JACKSON, VAN BUREN, AND THE TREATY OF NEW ECHOTA 28
CHAPTER 6: ATTACKING THE MUSCOGEE (CREEK) 36
CHAPTER 7: THE ORIGINAL DEATH MARCH? THE TRAIL OF TEARS 40
CHAPTER 8: LEGAL IMPLICATIONS AND REBUILDING THE CHEROKEE TRIBE 50
CHAPTER 9: HISTORICAL LEGACY 55
CHAPTER 10: LEGENDARY FIGURES 63
CHAPTER 11: NATIVE AMERICAN REMOVAL: A TIMELINE 83
CONCLUSION 92
AFTERWORD 93
HERE'S ANOTHER BOOK BY ENTHRALLING HISTORY THAT YOU MIGHT LIKE 97
FREE LIMITED TIME BONUS 98
BIBLIOGRAPHY 99

Introduction

This book tells the story of the clash between the Native American tribes that occupied the southeastern part of the United States during the 1800s and the European settlers who originally came to America to escape religious persecution. Due to their lust for land and profit, wealthy "land-jobbers" (land speculators) lured settlers westward, decimating the Native Americans who were in their path. Many treaties were made with the US government, some by tribal agreement, some by dissidents who claimed to speak for the entire tribe, and some by unscrupulous gold diggers and land-grabbers backed by corrupt politicians who wanted the land for themselves.

Often, when the settlers broke the treaties and occupied Native American land, the government overlooked these violations, hoping to avoid a conflict with the states. Given the subsequent Native American resistance to the encroachment of their lands and the response by state militias and the US military, along with the resulting massacre and displacement of many tribes, we must ask ourselves, "Was this death and destruction of the American Indian nations inevitable? Could the Native Americans and the settlers have gotten along with mutual concern for each other's well-being while sharing the land?

These are the questions that will be pondered in this book, and they revolve around the age-old question of human greed, to which there may be no answer.

Chapter 1: The Five Civilized Tribes

The Cherokee

Any story involving the Native American tribes must begin with those that have been titled the Five Civilized Tribes, those hard-working farmers and herders who mostly lived in the Southern US states. These tribes were the Cherokee, Choctaw, Muscogee (Creeks), Chickasaw, and Seminole. They earned their name because they adopted American culture more readily than other tribes, leading them to be seen as "civilized" in the eyes of the US government.

As a note, what follows is a very brief overview of the tribes, so we encourage you to learn more about their cultures. The best way to begin your research is to visit local Native American museums and cultural centers.

We will begin with the Cherokee Nation, the largest tribe in America today. They put up the fiercest resistance to the government's attempts to displace them from their ancestral homelands.

The Cherokee were an ethnic group bound together by kinship (clans) whose members spoke the Iroquoian language. They had villages in northern Georgia in the Blue Ridge Mountains and, to a lesser extent, on the Upper Savannah River. They had extensive relations, albeit not always friendly, with the Creek and the Sappony, who lived in the Piedmont area on the North Carolina-Virginia border. The Cherokee was the most populous tribe east of the Mississippi, and their clans were spread across the Carolinas, Georgia, Alabama, and Tennessee.[1]

A Cherokee nation was a confederacy of towns under a supreme war chief or a supreme peace chief. The natives in the red (war) towns were under the supreme war chief, and the natives in the white (peace) towns were ruled by, you guessed it, the supreme peace chief.

The Cherokee, like many other tribes, banded together to fight the encroachment of white settlers. However, they had a unique system of beliefs, including the Bear Dance (Yona), where they danced around a fire or pot with gourd and tortoise shell rattles.

Another thing that distinguished the Cherokee from other tribes was the fact they tended to side with the British in trade and war, which brought them into conflict with the colonies when they expanded westward. Since the colonists were encroaching on Native American land, they denied the natives access to their hunting grounds, in effect destroying the economic sustenance upon which they relied. The Cherokee were drawn into several wars by the British. For instance, they fought against the Yamasee in 1715 in South Carolina, which led to a forty-year war between the Cherokee and the Creeks.[2]

However, by 1759 the British and Cherokee were at each other's throats. Open warfare broke out since the Cherokee felt they had not been rewarded for their efforts in aiding the British against the French and other Native American tribes. During the Anglo-Cherokee War (1758-1761), each side accused the other of betrayals during the French and Indian War. The British burned villages and slaughtered the Cherokee, and the Cherokee attacked settlers.

With the Treaty of Long Island of Holston (1777), a temporary peace ensued, as the Cherokee were given Long Island in exchange

---

[1] Boulware, Tyler. "Cherokee Indians." *New Georgia Encyclopedia*, 20 January 2009, https://www.georgiaencyclopedia.org/articles/history-archaeology/cherokee-indians/.
[2] Ibid.

for giving up their claims in east Tennessee. Eventually, the Cherokee again sided with the British against the colonists, only to be persecuted and slaughtered by Southern militias. A brave Cherokee warrior named Dragging Canoe continued the fight after numerous treaties were violated and more land was lost. For ten years after the American Revolution, Dragging Canoe led the Chickamauga Cherokees in a last-ditch effort to work with the British and other Native American tribes, but the Cherokee warriors were ultimately forced to give up the fight.

The "Federal Road," the main road from southern Georgia to Knoxville, Tennessee, was the gateway to the West. In his second term, President George Washington designated this as a westward mail route, but by 1806, under the Tellico Treaty, the Cherokee were paid $1,600 to ferry travelers through Cherokee territory. In time, the settlers encroached on the Cherokee lands, thereby wiping out their hunting grounds, which eventually led to their displacement in Oklahoma.[3]

Prior to this removal, many Cherokee chiefs resisted the removal efforts, pointing to the Treaty of Hopewell (1785), which laid out the boundaries between the US and the Cherokee Confederacy. Cherokee Chief John Ross led the resistance group known as the Cherokee Triumvirate, which consisted of himself, Charles Hicks, and Major Ridge. Together, they crafted the Treaty of 1819, in which the government aided Cherokees who agreed to give up land in the Southeast for land west of the Mississippi.

The" Peace Party," those Cherokee leaders who wanted the Cherokee Nation to move to Oklahoma, went against the wishes of Chief John Ross by negotiating the Treaty of New Echota in 1835, which agreed to the removal of all Cherokee beyond the Mississippi. Those dissident Cherokees, led by Major Ridge, who had earlier sided with John Ross, would later pay the price for his fraudulent actions. His son, John Ridge, and nephew, Elias Boudinot, who also signed the treaty, would also lose their lives.

Thus, the Cherokee Nation ceased to exist as a unified body in the American Southeast due to warfare, starvation, disease, and loss of economic sustenance. After several years of disagreements with

---

[3] Ibid.

the Peace Party and the Cherokee Triumvirate, those who had not already left ultimately agreed to relocate to Oklahoma. John Ross traveled to Washington, DC, to negotiate the withdrawal of the remaining Cherokee, and the federal government provided them with two million dollars for their journey west.

The Choctaw

The Choctaw originated from Mexico and western America and lived in the Mississippi River Valley along the Old Natchez Trace Forest Trail, which was the main trading route between the eastern and southern frontiers. This area, the Southeast Woodland areas of Alabama, Mississippi, and Louisiana, was the homeland of this Muskogean tribe of warriors.

Their life was centered around agriculture. The Choctaw grew corn and beans, which they traded with other tribes, the Europeans, and the Americans. They played stickball and chunky stone (*tchungkee*), which they used to "prepare for war or as an alternative to war." In the game of chunky stone, disk-shaped stones were rolled across the ground. Then, the players threw spears to see who could get the closest.[4]

Another interesting fact about the Choctaw is that they found flat heads attractive. One of their customs was to tie a board or bag of sand to a child's head at birth to flatten the skull until it became elongated like a football.

The Choctaw were known for having a matriarchal society and their elaborate celebration of the harvest, known as the Green Corn Festival. The Choctaw diet included fish, corn, squash, deer, bear, nuts, and beans. All of these commodities were valuable trading assets.

Like the Cherokee, the Choctaw were skilled traders, warriors, and consumers, but unfortunately, they, too, met the same fate as the other tribes who were displaced. The Choctaw aligned themselves with the British in the 1700s and 1800s for trade and security connections, but in the process, they became involved in wars against other tribes. Eventually, they sided with the French to decimate the Natchez tribe.

---

[4] "Early Choctaw History." https://www.nps.gov/natr/learn/historyculture/choctaw.htm.

Chief Pushmataha was the most famous Choctaw. He fought with the Americans in the War of 1812 and negotiated treaties with the US government. However, in the end, it was all in vain. The monopolistic land speculators from the Northeast began selling land parcels in the Mississippi Valley, luring settlers to the area, which caused them to clash with the Choctaw.

Pushmataha was honored as a brigadier general of the US Army and buried in the Congressional Cemetery.
https://commons.wikimedia.org/wiki/File:Pushmataha_high_resolution.jpg

After President Andrew Jackson passed the Indian Removal Act of 1830, seventy thousand Choctaw walked the Trail of Tears, which went through Georgia, Tennessee, Mississippi, and Arkansas. The Choctaw were rounded up and placed in camps with little time for packing belongings, so they often had no blankets or shoes. The supply outposts charged high prices and were often raided by settlers. The Cherokee were better prepared, as they had doctors and supply depots along the way, but the journey to Oklahoma was still arduous. Around four thousand Cherokees and about three thousand Choctaws died along the way. It should be noted that the numbers of deaths vary wildly from source to source; we have chosen to go with the most agreed-upon numbers in this book.

Muscogee (Creek)

Like the Cherokee and the Choctaw, the Creek was also a warrior tribe, although there was more to these tribes than warfare. One of the most notable Creek leaders was Chief Menawa, meaning

"The Great Warrior," who led his Red Stick fighters (those who carried red-painted war clubs) during the Battle of Horseshoe Bend (modern-day Alabama) in 1814 and in the fight against General Andrew Jackson's troops at Enitichopco Creek.

Menawa was the chief of Okfuskee and owned large herds of cattle and hogs. He traded horses and pelts with people in Pensacola but eventually became incensed by the encroachment of Creek lands in Georgia and Alabama by the settlers. Menawa began raiding settlements and towns to steal horses, which brought him into conflict with General Jackson's forces at Horseshoe Bend.[5]

The Creek, like the Cherokee to the north and Choctaw to the east, were agricultural tribes. They cultivated corn, beans, squash, pumpkins, melons, and sweet potatoes. They also had a manufacturing company in Columbus, Georgia, where they made baskets, pottery, and colorful deerskins. The Creek also traded beeswax, hides, furs, honey, and venison.

The Creek Confederacy became splintered after Jackson defeated them at Horseshoe Bend and forced them to cede half of Alabama. Jackson's role in the Battle of Horseshoe Bend helped propel him to the presidency, where he enacted a law that moved the Southeastern tribes west of the Mississippi. An estimated 3,500 Creeks died on the Trail of Tears.[6]

The Chickasaw: Chikasha-Saya ("I am Chickasaw")

The Chickasaw had a great love of tattoos (war paint), which they believed enhanced their warrior spirit. The Chickasaw were ferocious warriors and were known as the "Spartans of the Mississippi." They participated in many battles with other tribes and against the white settlers.[7] They lived in Mississippi, Alabama, Tennessee, and Kentucky until 1832, when they were forced to move to Oklahoma.

Like the Cherokee, Choctaw, and Creek, the Chickasaw was an agricultural nation that carried out trade with the British and French,

---

[5] Braund, Kathryn. "Menawa." http://encyclopediaofalabama.org/article/h-3594

[6] Haveman, Christopher. "Creek Indian Removal." http://encyclopediaofalabama.org/article/h-2013.

[7] "History: Chickasaw Nation." https://www.chickasaw.net/our-nation/history.aspx

but in many ways, they were different from the other Civilized Tribes. They had a network of towns in Alabama, Kentucky, and Tennessee, and their capital was in Tishomingo, Mississippi. The Chickasaw established laws, religion, a constitution with a legislative and executive branch, and popular elections.

We are told they fought with the French against the British in the French and Indian War and that the Chickasaw Mounted Regiment ultimately aided the South in the Civil War. Following the war, they became successful farmers and ranchers while building schools, banks, and businesses in Native American territory.

The Doaksville Treaty of 1837 sealed this semi-nomadic tribe's fate. The Chickasaw was the last of the Five Civilized Tribes forced by the US government to travel on the Trail of Tears. Between five hundred to one thousand Chickasaw died on the journey.

The Seminole

The Seminole arrived in what is now called Florida long before the Spanish. The Spanish called them "*Cimarrones*," which means "wild ones" or "runaways" due to the Seminoles constantly eluding capture. The tribe had members across Florida, Georgia, and Alabama, and they designated themselves as unconquered people who sought freedom from conquest.[8]

The Seminoles traded with the Spanish, and in turn, the Spanish bought leather and cattle from them. The Seminoles were known for sewing, patchwork, chickee building (a type of log cabin building), and alligator wrestling. They lived in palm-thatched houses (chickees), wore ornamental clothing, celebrated the passing of the seasons, and practiced their ancestral forms of music and dance.[9]

One of their great warrior chiefs was Abiaka, a war chief of the Panther Clan. He was considered a great medicine man who became chief when others were too old or had emigrated. Abiaka, also known as Sam Jones, led his warriors deep into the swamps, where they could successfully fight the American soldiers. Abiaka was the chief of the Miccosukee (a Seminole-Creek tribe) and

---

[8] "Introduction." https://www.semtribe.com/stof/history/introduction .
[9] "Seminole History." https://dos.myflorida.com/florida-facts/florida-history/seminole-history/

guided his people through the swamps during the many decades of warfare. They shadowed the American soldiers as they navigated the swamps, so the US soldiers were constantly subjected to surprise attacks. Although the swamps were rife with disease, Abiaka was knowledgeable in medicinal herbs, saving the lives of his men numerous times.[10]

Abiaka used guerrilla warfare or hit-and-run tactics to fight the American soldiers. A cook named Martha Jane stated that at a meeting with a US general in 1847, Abiaka supposedly said, "My mother died [here], my father died here, and be damned I die here too." His resistance to moving to where the white settlers wanted him to go was so strong that he supposedly killed his sister when she thought about emigrating. He was so hateful toward the white settlers that he often threw down the money offered to him and refused to even look at them.

Due to his determination and skill as a great medicine man and leader, Abiaka was never captured, no matter how hard General Zachary Taylor, the last general who pursued him, tried. Abiaka eventually died in the swamps he loved.[11]

About five hundred Seminoles remained in Florida after the fighting, as the US grew weary of its war with the tribe since no real progress was being made. However, many Seminoles either left willingly or were forced to leave.

---

[10] "Abiaka (Seminole Indian Sam Jones) - One of the Greatest Medicine Men in History." https://worldprophesy.blogspot.com/2015/01/abiaka-one-of-greatest-medicine-men-seminole.html.

[11] Ibid.

Chapter 2: Sinister Origins

With this basic background on the Five Civilized Tribes, we can begin to understand the clash of civilizations that took place in America between 1810 and 1860, a clash that affected more than just five tribes. The element of greed came into play, as the white settlers desired the natives' land. Speculators trespassed on Native American lands, searching for gold, and negotiated contracts to build railroads. Swamps were drained, and canals were dug, all at the expense of the Native American tribes, who lost their hunting grounds and were forced to flee into the swamps and woodlands of North America.

It did not matter that the Native Americans were becoming Europeanized. Christianity was becoming more and more prevalent, displacing indigenous religions. Some tribes that had previously depended on hunting were now farming, and many were developing different forms of government. Meanwhile, the settlers were pushing westward at a rapid pace, bulldozing anything or anyone in their path. The wealthy speculators and the state governments, with the tacit approval of the federal government, enriched themselves in the process.

The quote that Yosemite Sam yelled to Bugs Bunny says it all: "There's gold in them thar hills!" Gold led to the encroachment of Native American lands by gold diggers and wealthy capitalists who sought land for their enterprises. Many historians cite General William Tecumseh Sherman's search for gold in California as igniting the Gold Rush, which, in turn, led to a gold rush on Native American lands from the Dakotas to California.

The clash between the Native Americans and the incoming settlers seemed inevitable, given the arrival of the Europeans and the "greed" inherent in the quest for material wealth. But how were the Native Americans treated before the Trail of Tears?

As we noted earlier, the Seminoles were in America before the Spanish, and they were probably the first to face the encroachment of their lands by the conquistadors led by Ponce de León and Hernando de Soto. However, that story is for another day. A good place to begin our tale would be with the Treaty of Hopewell in 1785, which was signed under the presidency of John Hancock, who was president of the Second Continental Congress. This treaty between the Cherokee, Choctaw, and Chickasaw and the United States government was signed in South Carolina. Under the terms of the treaty, the Native Americans gave up sections of their lands in return for protection. The treaty was soon violated by the encroaching settlers, and the tribal leaders refused to recognize the sovereignty of the United States or the states in which they lived.

A few years later, in 1791, President George Washington, like Andrew Jackson forty years later, made the "Indian problem" a top priority. He wanted a just policy, and like President Jackson, he may have been sincere in his wish for peace. However, in both cases, peace was not in the cards.[12]

Washington, who was purchasing large tracts of land, instructed the Administration of Indian Affairs to follow the "great principles of justice and humanity," but the administration soon learned the Continental Congress had already angered the Native Americans by ordering them to move west of the Mississippi. Secretary of War Henry Knox's opinion was expressed in his official report of June 15th, 1789, in which he "urged adoption of what he believed to be a just and humane policy that recognized Indian rights to the soil, rejected the principle of conquest, and compensated the Indians for lands they ceded."[13] But in a 1790 letter to Washington, he

---

[12] "Native Americans." https://www.mountvernon.org/george-washington/native-americans/ .

[13] "Report of Henry Knox on the Northwestern Indians." https://pages.uoregon.edu/mjdennis/courses/hist469_Knox.htm.

apparently changed his mind, saying, "it is incumbent on the United States to be in a position to punish all unprovoked aggressions."[14] This put the administration in a conundrum, and Washington eventually came to believe the Native Americans would be better off if they were separated from the white settlers.

President Washington decided the constitutional power of treaty-making, which was to be carried out between the Senate and the president, should be applied to the Native Americans.

When the Shawnee, Miami, Ottawa, Chippewa, Iroquois, Fox, and Souk in the Ohio Valley decided they were giving up too much land, they began to resist removal. The president sent in five thousand troops under General "Mad" Anthony Wayne to put down the rebellion. In the Battle of Fallen Timbers (1794), the Native American confederation was destroyed. The Treaty of Greenville (1795) led to a period of peace, allowing Washington to turn his attention south to deal with the problems between Georgia and the Creek, Chickasaw, Choctaw, and Cherokee, four of the so-called "Civilized Tribes."

The Creeks disagreed with the three treaties they had signed with Georgia since they had been forced to cede twenty-three million acres (part of southern Georgia and half of Alabama). A delegation of twenty-eight chiefs traveled to New York for the negotiations, and under the Treaty of New York, they recovered some of their lands taken by Georgia. But the stipulations the Washington administration included in the treaty involved more than just peace. The treaty protected the Creeks in Georgia but also stated they should become "acculturated and civilized" while becoming part of land settlements where they would be subject to state laws.

Washington's thinking from his early experience with Native Americans led him to believe the natives should be Europeanized, as it would allow them to blend in easier with white society and overcome the prejudices they faced. As such, the treaty stipulated the Creeks should give up hunting and become "herdsmen and cultivators."

---

[14] Knox, Henry. "To George Washington from Henry Knox." https://founders.archives.gov/documents/Washington/05-04-02-0353.

But again, as we glance into the future, George Washington had the same problem as Andrew Jackson and Martin Van Buren: an overwhelming influx of white settlers moving toward the western frontier. This is a fact that critics of the Native Americans' removal do not take into consideration when they castigate Andrew Jackson, who is often accused of genocide due to his Native American removal policies. An argument can certainly be made for blaming the settlers, the land speculators, the greedy, cutthroat railroad barons, and those who pushed for the expansion and growth of the United States to build it into an empire. Typically, though, the bulk of the blame is generally placed on President Jackson and Van Buren, the latter of which continued Jackson's policies.

Even back in 1776, Washington and Knox were afraid the Native American tribes would be annihilated by the throng of settlers, with Washington saying, "I believe scarcely anything short of a Chinese Wall, or a line of troops will restrain land jobbers and the encroachment of settlers upon the Indian territory."[15] So, if we want to talk about genocide or the sinister origins of the removal of Native Americans, we have to start with the white settlers and westward expansion. However, the doublespeak of politicians, along with the bribes they took from wealthy speculators, should not be overlooked either.

American historian Colin Calloway looks at the darker side of George Washington to sort of dull the shine of his American armor. As we said, Washington, like Jackson, opposed Native American removal and claimed he wanted to treat them humanely by allowing them to remain on their lands if they agreed to recognize the power of the state in which they resided, which, of course, forced them to deny their own sovereignty. Calloway argues against the idea that Washington knew that Native American removal was "inevitable" by stating that "Washington knew that he must build his nation on Indian land, and by war and diplomacy ... knowing that westward expansion pushed Indians out and turned tribal homelands into States." He says Washington's goals were first to acquire land and then to seek justice for the Native Americans. If they refused to sell,

---

[15] Genovese, Michael A. & Landry, Alysa. *US Presidents and the Destruction of the Native American Nations (The Evolving American Presidency)*. Palgrave Macmillian, 2021.

Washington was willing to wage war on them. Calloway says that Washington used the word "extirpate," which means "destroy." He extirpated the Iroquois, who, in turn, called him "Town Destroyer."[16]

We are told by other historians that Washington often invited Native American chiefs to dine with him at his home in Philadelphia. Calloway tells us that after one of these meetings with Mohawk Chief Joseph Brant, Brant warned other Native Americans that Washington talked with a forked tongue. "George Washington is very cunning, he will try to fool us if he can. He speaks very smooth, will tell you fair stories, and at the same time want to ruin us."

He further noted that the Treaty of New York contained six "secret articles" that the Creek were not aware of when they signed the treaty with the US, but only two were ratified by the Senate. Less than a year later, Washington sent troops to destroy Native American villages in northwest Ohio because they refused to cede their ancestral land. Calloway summarizes his essay by saying that "Washington's decisions set precedents that are still with us. As the father of the country, he was also the father of America's tortuous, conflicted, and often hypocritical Indian policies."[17]

In 1811, General William Henry Harrison, the future US president, defeated Shawnee Chief Tecumseh and the Northwest tribes in the Battle of Tippecanoe in Indiana, dashing Tecumseh's hope for a Northwest Confederacy. After this followed the War of 1812, in which many Native American tribes fought with the British. Another future president, General Andrew Jackson, called "Sharp Knife" by the Native Americans because of his cruelty, battled the Red Stick warriors of the Creeks. Ultimately, twenty-three million acres of Creek land were confiscated.

Finally, in 1830, President Jackson sponsored the Indian Removal Act, which eventually forced the remaining tribes, including the Seminoles of Florida, who had already ceded four

---

[16] Calloway, Colin. "George Washington Lived in an Indian World, but His Biographies Have Erased Native People." https://longreads.com/2018/11/07/george-washington-lived-in-an-indian-world-but-his-biographies-have-erased-native-people.

[17] Ibid.

million acres under the treaty of Moultrie in 1823, west of the Mississippi. The Seminoles in Florida were attacked by the militias of Georgia and the US Army and were pushed farther south into the swamps. This was due to the competitive nature of their farming and because Native American tribes were using runaway slaves for their farms, which the plantations needed to cultivate their crops. The Seminoles continued to resist even after the Indian Removal Act was passed. The act ultimately resulted in the Second Seminole War (1835-1842), which was followed by the Third Seminole War of 1855, after which the Seminole population in Florida was reduced to only a few hundred.

The population explosion in the United States made westward expansion a necessity for the settlers, who were being lured by land speculators. The clash between land speculators and Native Americans occurred because the speculators viewed Native Americans as a stumbling block on the path to social and economic development. The idea of Manifest Destiny brought with it opportunities for farming, raising cattle, and logging. As such, the idea of Manifest Destiny, the idea that expansion was divinely ordained and justifiable, led to the removal of Native Americans from their ancestral homelands.

Emanuel Gottlieb Leutze, Westward the Course of Empire Takes Its Way (mural study, US Capitol), 1861, oil on canvas, Smithsonian American Art Museum, Bequest of Sara Carr Upton, 1931.
https://commons.wikimedia.org/wiki/File:Westward_the_Course_of_Empire.jpg

Historically, many prominent Americans, such as President George Washington and President James Madison, advocated westward expansion. Of course, President Andrew Jackson (1829-1837), President Martin Van Buren (1837-1841), and President James Polk (1845-1849) supported the idea of Manifest Destiny, a term coined by newspaper editor John O'Sullivan around 1845.

The explosion of Europeans arriving on the East Coast, the land speculators who pushed them westward, and the gold rush all contributed to the move to push the Native American tribes out of their homelands.

Chapter 3: The Indian Removal Act 1830: Cause and Consequence

While many factors led to the removal of the Native Americans from their ancestral lands, Leonard Carlson and Mark Roberts, in their article titled "Indian Lands, Squatterism, and Slavery," tell us that the Southern slaveholders wanted more land in the west to grow cotton, while Northern manufacturers, led by the Whig Party, felt that expanding westward would be detrimental to businesses in New England. The dispute raged in Congress.

Meanwhile, President Andrew Jackson considered the Indian Removal Act. Squatters had settled on Native American lands and demanded to be allowed to buy the land they occupied at a low cost. Georgia, which had a large Cherokee population, demanded the tribes that had a claim to Georgian lands be removed to the west to preserve their culture and prevent their annihilation at the hands of the settlers and state militias.[18]

---

[18] Carlson, Leonard A., and Mark A. Roberts. "Indian Lands, Squatterism, and Slavery: Economic Interests and the Passage of the Indian Removal Act of 1830." *Explorations in Economic History* 43.3 (2006): 486-504. Web. www.sciencedirect.com.ezproxy.liberty.edu.

The Indian Removal Act gave President Jackson the authority to exchange lands west of the Mississippi for lands the Native Americans were living on within state borders. In the late 1830s, the government began to forcibly move the Cherokees and other tribes west via what came to be known as the Trail of Tears.

There were some people who were against the Indian Removal Act, including Congressman Davey Crockett, who declared his vote against it would "not make me ashamed in the day of judgement."[19] Christian Missionary and newspaper publisher Jerimiah Evarts used his newspaper to oppose the act. Cherokee Chief John Ross traveled many times to Washington, DC, to argue against it as well.

As a boy, Davey Crockett grew up in the wild frontier of present-day eastern Tennessee. After several skirmishes with schoolmates and reprimands by his father, the strong-willed boy ran away from home at the age of fourteen, working as a hatmaker and a cattle driver. In 1813, he joined the Tennessee militia in the fight against the Red Stick faction of the Creeks. The Red Sticks fought other Creeks and the US government, as they were vehemently opposed to becoming assimilated by the Americans. They had carried out a massacre at Fort Mims, Alabama, where hundreds of civilians were killed or captured. During the Creek War, Crockett was a scout and a game hunter but was with General Andrew Jackson when the latter massacred over two hundred Red Sticks at the Creek settlement of Tallahatchie.

Davy Crockett was elected to Congress in 1827 after a bout in the state legislature, and he used his sharp tongue to oppose Jackson's Indian Removal Act in 1830, which he voted against. In an 1834 letter, he lambasted Jackson's forced removal of the Cherokee to Oklahoma and lamented the notion that Vice President Martin Van Buren would carry out Jackson's Native American policies. Crockett threatened to move to the "wilds of Texas" if Van Buren was elected. Due to Crockett's angry opposition to Jackson's Native American policies, he was voted out of office in 1835. Angry at his loss, he uttered his famous statement, "You may all go to hell, but I

---

[19] "Davy Crockett on the Removal of the Cherokees, 1834."
https://www.gilderlehrman.org/history-resources/spotlight-primary-source/davy-crockett-removal-cherokees-1834.

will go to Texas." And that is what he did, eventually dying during the Battle of the Alamo in 1836.

In spite of vehement opposition across the country, the vote in Congress was 102 to 97, with the Senate concurring. Almost all of the Five Civilized Tribes were pressured to move west. Not everyone went along peacefully, as they did not want to leave their home. Consequently, the state militias and the government responded with military force. Forty-six thousand Native Americans were forcibly removed from their homes. Thousands died of disease and starvation.[20]

As the violence continued, many Americans who originally opposed relocation and favored assimilation came to agree with those who supported it, not just for economic reasons but also for humanitarian ones. Abolitionists, ministers, Quakers, Baptists, Methodists, and other Christians argued that Native Americans should be moved west to preserve their culture and ensure they wouldn't be exterminated by the settlers.

A year before the Indian Removal Act was passed (1829), during the contentious congressional debate over the act, a playwright named John August Stone wrote *Metamora or The Last of the Wampanoags*, a play that portrayed the conflict between the Puritans and the Wampanoags in the 1600s. It features a Wampanoag named Metamora as a scorned and violent "savage" who declares war against the English settlers. In the end, he kills his wife to protect her from the white invaders, after which the Wampanoags are slaughtered by the settlers. (In reality, the Wampanoags were decimated by smallpox and conflicts in the 1600s. Their numbers were at around seven thousand in 1610 but dipped to around four hundred only seventeen years later.)

Historians debate whether this play, which was popular in New England, added fuel to the fire in the debate to displace the Native Americans, especially since the story resonated with what was going on at the time. President Jackson signed the Indian Removal Act into law only a year after the play came out. Others contend that Stone was taking advantage of the climate at the time and used

---

[20] "May 28, 1830 CE: Indian Removal Act."
https://education.nationalgeographic.org/resource/indian-removal-act.

romantic ideals to create a popular work.

Nevertheless, most scholars recognize the importance of *Metamora*, such as historian Donald B. Grose in his article "Edwin Forest, 'Metamora,' and the Indian Removal Act of 1830." The play was released at a critical time in American history and portrayed a noble Native American caught up in the battle against white settlers encroaching on Native American land. Grose writes that it was a struggle forced upon the Native Americans by the War of 1812, which "brought on powerful nationalism and egalitarianism in the United States." The play displays "the sentiment for removal and the final solution; the removal of the Native Americans to prevent their annihilation."[21]

The play was written for a contest that Edwin Forrest, an actor, had created to find a play based on a Native American character. Stone won the prize money. Forrest based his interpretation of the character on a Choctaw named Pushmataha, whom he had met years before. Stone based the character on King Philip or Chief Metacom, who fought against the English in King Philip's War.

---

[21] Grose, B. Donald. "Edwin Forrest, 'Metamora,' and the Indian Removal Act of 1830." *Theatre Journal*, vol. 37, no. 2, 1985, pp. 181-91. *JSTOR*, https://doi.org/10.2307/3207064. Accessed 18 Sep. 2022.

Edwin Forrest as Metamora in 1829.
(Internet Book Archives Images, no restrictions.
https://commons.wikimedia.org/wiki/File:The_autobiography_of_Joseph_Jefferson_(1890)_(14778655621).jpg)

Metamora played in theaters around the nation and reflected the ambivalence of many concerning Native American removal, as well as the struggle between northeastern humanitarians who favored assimilation and federal and state officials who felt it better to separate the Native Americans and the white man.

Grose puts the play in context by stating the "timeliness of the script about contemporary white-Indian affairs cannot be disallowed, for the play and Forrest were caught up in twenty years of white expansion at the expense of the Indian's lands and rights." The protagonist in the play, Metamora, "sees heroic immortality in defeat: 'We are destroyed—now vanquished; we are no more, yet we are forever.'" Grose states the play portrays all the noble characteristics of the "savage," as well as the opposing traits of the "red devil."[22]

With its foundation in Renaissance primitivism, the stereotype of the noble savage exemplified the Native American as a person of physical beauty and natural grace, filled with an intuitive knowledge of nature and its secrets. The noble savage was elegant of speech, stoic, and loyal to friends, relatives, and loved ones. When this stereotype was brought into conflict with the other version of Native Americans, the "red devil," those who only sought out violence and the destruction of the white civilization, people were uncertain how to balance the two sides of the coin. To most, three methods were possible: willing victimization, acculturation, and extermination.

And therein lies the crux of the complex struggle between the Native Americans and white settlers that took place in the United States between 1830 and 1850, although it had started well before. The situation was more complex than most realize, and *Metamora* is a good example of the way Native Americans were shown. The play shows "the Indian who via acculturation ... rejects Indianness and becomes a white ... but is unwilling to acknowledge his inferiority ad later becomes a diabolical savage, the red devil." Grose tells us the stereotype also fulfills the European conceptualization of the wild man of folklore. "His savagery grew as much as out of his failure to be white as of out of his deeds, for the red devil has the opportunity to be a white and rejects it with force."[23]

Finally, Grose notes that *Metamora* fits in with the idea of Manifest Destiny and that it portrays all the racial concepts of the Native Americans at the time: nomadic, violent, treacherous, sadistic, and cowardly, allowing audiences in the 19th century to cheer Metamora on as a noble savage while at the same time making them look forward to his destruction.

In her article, "The Assimilation, Removal, and Elimination of American Indians," Jessica Keating of Notre Dame University further expands on the idea of assimilation, an idea she says was

---

[22] Ibid.
[23] Ibid.

developed out of the Enlightenment movement of the 18th century. She agrees with Grose that it was related to the notion of Manifest Destiny, the belief that America had the divine right to progress and expand westward. But the major obstacle to expansion was the Native American tribes that were occupying and blocking the lands needed for that progress. And as resistance continued, the government passed the Indian Removal Act. Over the next few decades, the Native Americans were forcibly removed to reservations in Oklahoma.[24]

---

[24] Keating, Jessica. "The Assimilation, Removal, and Elimination of American Indians." *The McGraph Institute for Church Life*, (2020). https://mcgrath.nd.edu/assets/390540/expert_guide_on_the_assimilation_removal_and_elimination_of_native_americans.pdf.

Chapter 4: Seminole Resistance: This Means War

With Florida being handed over to Spain in 1783 under the Treaty of Paris, white settlers began emigrating to Florida to take advantage of the land grants the Spanish government was offering. However, this land was occupied by the Seminoles, who attacked the settlers. The problem was further exacerbated by the fact that escaped slaves sought refuge in Florida, as it was not yet part of the United States. They were being pursued by militias from Georgia that sought to capture runaway slaves while also seeking land and cattle.

In 1816, US soldiers attacked and destroyed a garrison that housed escaped slaves, killing 270 people. The Seminoles retaliated by attacking settlements along the Florida-Georgia border. The First Seminole War then broke out in 1817 after General Andrew Jackson and his forces destroyed the Seminole village of Fowltown. The Seminoles retaliated by attacking Fort Scott, killing forty-three men, women, and children. Jackson continued his attacks on Seminole villages along the Suwannee River, capturing St. Marks, a Spanish military post, and the Spanish town of Pensacola.

At this point, Spain realized that Florida was a burden. The Spanish knew they could no longer protect their settlements and signed the Transcontinental Treaty (also known as the Adams-Onís Treaty) in 1819, under which they ceded Florida to the US. The US government controlled the eastern part of the territory and two years later laid claim to West Florida, which had also been ceded under the treaty.[25]

The Treaty of Moultrie Creek, which was signed in 1823 by the Seminoles and the US, stated the Seminoles would be given financial aid and a reservation of four million acres in Central Florida if they agreed to capture and return escaped slaves and cede all claims to Florida. But by this time, the animosity between the Seminoles, who were attacking the settlers along the Georgia-Florida border, the Georgia militias, which were raiding Native American territories to retrieve runaway slaves, and the US military led by Andrew Jackson, which was attacking and burning Native American villages, was heating up. The treaty was ultimately violated by all sides.[26]

The Second Seminole War (1835-1842) began when an influential Seminole warrior named Osceola murdered an Indian agent named Wiley Thompson (he was originally from Virginia but served in the Georgia Senate). Osceola was named Billy Powell upon his birth. As an infant, he lived in Alabama with his Muscogee mother. His father was most likely a Scotsman named William Powell. Billy and his mother moved to Florida when he was a child. His family and other Creeks joined the Seminoles. As the years passed, the encroachment of white settlers continued to grow worse. After the Treaty of Moultrie Creek, many Seminoles, including Osceola (who got his name after joining the Seminoles), moved deeper into the unknown territories of Florida.

Together with other Seminole chiefs, such as Alligator, Jumper, Coacoochee, and Halleck-Tustennuggee, many Seminole warriors fought against the US military until their numbers began to decline. Many were killed, captured, or forcibly moved westward. In 1835, the Seminoles intensified the conflict by massacring a little over one hundred soldiers in an ambush near president-day Ocala. This was known as the Dade massacre, named after General Francis Dade, who led his soldiers through the swamps into an ambush. The Seminoles were hidden on higher ground, and General Dade was

---

[25] "The Seminole Wars." https://www.seminolenationmuseum.org/history/seminole-nation/the-seminole-wars/.

[26] Pauls, Elizabeth Prine. "Trail of Tears." Encyclopedia Britannica, 28 Mar. 2022, https://www.britannica.com/event/Trail-of-Tears. Accessed 24 August 2022.

the first one killed in the battle.

Osceola and Coacooche were captured in 1837 when General Jesup tricked the Seminoles under a false flag of truce.[27] A 1988 article in the South Florida *Sun Sentinel* says that Chief Osceola was taken on the SS *Poinsett* to a prison at Fort Moultrie, South Carolina, where he died. His doctor, Frederick Weedon, severed his head and took it home as a souvenir. But even with the capture and death of Chief Osceola, the Seminoles continued to resist.[28]

The Third Seminole War (1855-1858) was led by a Seminole chief named Holata Micco, who was called Billy Bowlegs by the white settlers and military. Legend says he became bowlegged from his love of riding Spanish horses. Holata Micco, which means "Alligator Chief," was the last remaining established Seminole chief to lead the resistance against white encroachment.[29] He led a band of two hundred warriors and eluded capture to the end.[30]

Though Holata Micco had signed the Treaty of Payne's Landing in 1832, which required all Seminoles to move west of the Mississippi, he refused to leave Florida, saying that he was born there and that he would die there. After the treaty, Holata Micco and his family lived in peace until surveyors and engineers destroyed his banana trees. To him, it was clear the settlers would not stop and that violence was the only answer. He waged a guerrilla war against the US Army, which, in turn, attacked Seminole villages and tracked warriors with bloodhounds.

Three thousand Seminoles had already been deported via boat from New Orleans, and the pressure was intensifying to remove the rest of them to Oklahoma. Desperate to subdue the Alligator Chief, the government sent Chief Wild Cat of the Western Seminoles to urge the defiant Bowlegs to relocate to Indian Territory. Bowlegs was offered ten thousand dollars and one thousand dollars each for

---

[27] "The Seminole Wars." https://www.seminolenationmuseum.org/history/seminole-nation/the-seminole-wars/.

[28] McIver, Stuart. "Bring Me the Head of Osceola." *Sun Sentinel*. https://www.sun-sentinel.com/news/fl-xpm-1988-01-31-8801070155-story.html.

[29] "Third Seminole War." https://www.u-s-history.com/pages/h1156.html

[30] African American Registry (AAREG), "Billy Bowlegs, Seminole Chief." https://osceolahistory.org/billy-bowlegs-iii-ahead-of-his-time/.

his chiefs. He did not agree at first, but after his camp was destroyed in 1857, he bowed to the inevitable and changed his mind several months later.

In 1858, Bowlegs and nearly two hundred other Seminoles finally surrendered. That December, he returned to convince the last of the Seminoles to move west. The vast majority of Seminoles did not walk the Trail of Tears but were taken by boat from New Orleans to the west.

In 1859, Holata Micco (Billy Bowlegs) arrived in the territory of Arkansas with his two wives, one son, five daughters, and fifty slaves. Freed blacks lived in Seminole communities and served as advisors, hunters, warriors, and interpreters. But as part of the process of assimilation into American-European culture, the Five Civilized Tribes adopted slavery. In most cases, they were forced to give up their slaves when they were deported, but Bowlegs was allowed to keep his slaves.

After the forcible removal of Bowlegs and his family, there were still a couple of hundred Seminoles who refused to leave Florida. They lived in isolation until the late 1920s.

Chapter 5: Manifest Destiny: Jackson, Van Buren, and the Treaty of New Echota

Andrew Jackson, the future military hero and popular Democratic president, started his climb to the top at the age of thirteen when he was arrested in 1781 by the British for refusing to polish a British officer's boots. As time went on, his mother died from cholera while tending to wounded soldiers in the War of 1812. Meanwhile, his hatred of the British intensified. Jackson became a lawyer and moved from the South Carolina-Georgia border to Tennessee, where he became a wealthy landowner. He was elected to the House of Representatives, then the Senate, and, for a while, he was a judge. His popularity led to his appointment as major general of the Tennessee Militia. Jackson fought in the war against the British in 1812, where he won the Battle of New Orleans, ironically with the help of Choctaw warriors.[31]

In 1814, with about three thousand US soldiers and around six hundred Native American allies, Jackson fought the Red Stick faction of the Creeks, those who carried red-painted wooden clubs, a few months after they massacred settlers at Fort Mims, Alabama.

---

[31] Biography.com Editors. "Andrew Jackson Biography." *A&E Networks.* (2017). https://www.biography.com/us-president/andrew-jackson.

The Creeks themselves were divided, which is what led to the Creek War to begin with. The Red Sticks, led by Peter McQueen and William Weatherford, wanted to unite all the tribes in a war against the US, but the White Sticks under Big Warrior wanted peace.

The Creek War morphed into something larger as time passed, with the Red Sticks attacking white settlements. To put down this rebellion, the US sided with the White Stick warriors. The war culminated in the Battle of Horseshoe Bend, in which eight hundred Red Stick warriors were killed. The US government confiscated twenty-three million acres from the Creeks in Alabama and Georgia, even though many Creeks had fought against or were opposed to the Red Sticks.[32]

After Jackson's victory at New Orleans, his men nicknamed him "Old Hickory" for his toughness, and Jackson proved this nickname when he and his troops marched into Florida, which was still Spanish territory, and defeated the Seminoles at St. Marks and Pensacola in 1818. This essentially gave him control of the western part of Florida. In the 1819 Adams-Onís Treaty, Spain officially ceded the territory of Florida to the United States.

After reigning as territorial governor for two months, Jackson returned to Tennessee to begin his political career. In 1824, Senator Jackson was urged to run for the presidency, which would be the start of his war against what John Tyler called the "monied monopoly," i.e., the land speculators and their cronies in Congress who wanted a US central bank. They would profit from this venture since the bank could provide loans to them.

According to Thomas DiLorenzo, in his book *The Real Lincoln*, those who opposed Jackson split off from the Democratic-Republican Party to become the Whig-Republicans, while Jackson and his allies remained Democrats. His opponents labeled him a "jackass," and the president liked the name so much that it became the symbol of the Democratic Party.[33]

DiLorenzo tells us that Jackson was against the system of British mercantilism, which he felt was being forced on the US by advocates

---

[32] Ibid.

[33] DiLorenzo, Thomas. *The Real Lincoln: A New Look at Abraham Lincoln*. Crown Forum, 2003.

of a centralized government, under which Congress would subsidize corporations (corporate welfare). Jackson took James Madison's view that "the general welfare clause of the constitution was never intended to become a Pandora's Box for special interest legislation." Thus, we are told that when Jackson became president, he used his veto power to wipe out all internal improvement bills, referring to them as "saddling ... the government with the losses of unsuccessful private speculation." DiLorenzo further informs us that in Jackson's Farewell Address, he bragged that he had "finally overthrown ... this plan of unconstitutional expenditure for corrupt influence."[34]

Andrew Jackson was also against protectionist tariffs, which he felt favored big business, and he offered a bill to abolish the electoral college, as he was in favor of the popular vote. He also wanted to abolish the bureaucracy that remained in power when a new president was elected, allowing them to be replaced with loyal allies of the new president. In his battle against the Second Bank of the United States, which was the legacy of centralized government advocates like Alexander Hamilton and Henry Clay, Jackson tried to push a banking charter through Congress. President Jackson labeled the bank as a corrupt, elitist institution that manipulated paper money and had too much power over the economy. In 1836, he issued the Specie Circular, which required payment in gold and silver for the purchase of public lands.

Jackson won the battle in the end when the bank was boarded up, but after the death of President William Henry Harrison after only a year in office (1841), John Tyler continued the fight with the Whigs over whether a strong central government would be more beneficial than increased states' rights. This argument had caused President Jackson's vice president, John Calhoun, to resign when Jackson sided with South Carolina in the nullification crisis of 1832, in which South Carlina threatened to secede from the Union over high protectionist tariffs.

Jackson's views angered his opponents. A house painter attempted to shoot the president at a ceremony at the Capitol, but when the second gun didn't go off, Old Hickory rushed the man and beat him with his cane.

---

[34] Ibid.

Andrew Jackson is perhaps remembered best for the controversial Indian Removal Act of 1830, which led to the Trail of Tears. At the time, though, Jackson was a popular leader. However, the reality, according to Alfred Cave in his scholarly article, "Abuse of Power: Andrew Jackson and the Indian Removal Act of 1830," was that Jackson abused his power as president by not enforcing the treaties that already existed and by conniving with Democrat politicians, newspaper editors, state officials, and Indian agents to pass the Indian Removal Act.

In Jackson's mind, the Native Americans either lived in sovereign nations (which they claimed to be) or had to adhere to the state in which they lived. If they were sovereign nations, then they were not adhering to the Constitution and had to break apart.

According to Cave, the Indian Removal Act did not require the Native Americans to move; it gave them the choice of remaining on their lands if they recognized the states in which they lived. Cave claims the Indian Removal Act of 1830 "neither authorized the unilateral abrogation of treaties guaranteeing Native Americans land rights within the states, nor the forced relocation of the eastern Indians." In other words, the president passed the act off as if it required the Native Americans to relocate west, which it did not and was not what Congress intended, which Cave says was an "abuse of Presidential power." Hence, we are told that Jackson "disregarded a key section of the act" and also violated the Trade and Intercourse Act of 1802, which allowed white missionaries, teachers, and tradesmen to operate on Native American land.[35]

Jackson was under pressure from the American Board of Commissioners of Foreign Missions in Boston. This group was a thorn in Jackson's side, and he fought back by using the Trade and Intercourse Act of 1802 to deny missionaries access to Native American land. The act prohibited citizens from entering native territory without a license, and Jackson saw it as a way to prevent humanitarian groups from interfering with his policies regarding the Native American problem.

---

[35] Cave, Alfred A. "Abuse of Power: Andrew Jackson and the Indian Removal Act of 1830." *The Historian*, vol. 65, no. 6, 2003, pp. 1330-53. *JSTOR*, http://www.jstor.org/stable/24452618. Accessed 12 Sep. 2022.

Cave examined Jackson's December 1830 address to Congress, where he stated that emigration should be voluntary "for it would be unjust to compel the aborigines to abandon the graves of their fathers and seek a home in a distant land." This statement seems to show that Jackson changed his mind regarding Native American removal, claiming that states' rights were superior to federal power. Thus, he used states' rights as a ruse to avoid the issue and did nothing to protect the Cherokee from removal by Georgia officials, nor did he act against the state governments of Alabama and Mississippi when they moved the Choctaw to designated lands in the west.

Cave further argues that Jackson hid his push for Native American removal by following his predecessor's policy of granting lands west of the Mississippi to tribes willing to give up their lands. He notes the act provided $500,000 for Jackson to pay for improvements to houses, barns, and orchards but that no part of the act authorized the seizure of Native American lands that they did not cede via treaty.

Secretary of War John Henry Eaton informed Cherokee tribal leaders that their "[claim] of protected rights against encroachment by Georgia was nothing more than temporary grants of privilege awarded by a conquering power—the United States—to a vanquished people."[36] The secretary of war was essentially correct in saying that no treaty could be guaranteed. Ever since the population explosion and the subsequent westward push by settlers, squatters, gold diggers, and land speculators, buttressed by the pressure being put on President Jackson by state officials, made Native American removal almost inevitable. This argument counters Cave's argument that President Jackson abused his power. One can even argue that if he had removed white settlers from Native American lands, he might have caused the Civil War to start earlier than 1860. And furthermore, those in Congress who had the power to create treaties were just as responsible for violating the Indian Removal Act of 1830. Cave tells us the House Committee on Indian Affairs, although it was established by partisan Democrats, "dismissed Indian treaty-making as nothing more than an empty gesture to

---

[36] Ibid.

placate Indian vanity."[37]

According to Cave, Jackson urged his supporters, those in Congress and newspaper editors as well, to portray the act as providing for "voluntary removal" with "remuneration for ceded lands."

Democratic Representative Joseph Hemphill of Pennsylvania proposed an amendment that would have delayed action on the act for a year, pending the report of three impartial commissioners charged with discovering the real wishes of the tribes and certifying the suitability of the western lands designated for their use. But the act passed, with Northern Quakers and Democrats voting against it and most Southern Democrats voting for it.

It is important to put Cave's argument that President Jackson abused his power in the context of the social and political climate of the period. If Jackson had forcibly removed white settlers and squatters from Native American territories to enforce the treaties, this, along with his stand against South Carolina in the nullification act controversy, would have inflamed the states' rights factions that had already threatened to secede from the Union.

In summarizing his thesis on Jackson's usurpation of power, Cave points to the corruption in the removal program, but again, we can say the government was in a conundrum. Jackson could either forcibly relocate the Native Americans to territories west of the Mississippi or allow them to remain in the states, where they would likely be annihilated.

Thus, as we said in our introduction, greed was a major factor when it came to the Native Americans' removal, not only by corrupt officials in the government but also by Indian agents and, to a lesser extent, the chiefs and other Native Americans willing to accept money for themselves and for the resettlement of their tribe. A bit of history tells us that bureaucracies often ignore the wishes of their president and that the president is often between a rock and a hard place, which was certainly the case with President Jackson.

For those who say Jackson hated Native Americans, the context of the time makes it difficult to be certain. Perhaps he did. Or

---

[37] Ibid.

perhaps he was a pragmatist who believed the Native Americans would be better off if they relocated to faraway lands in Arkansas and Oklahoma, where their tribes could live in peace. In any case, the legacy of Jacksonian democracy and Native American hatred lives on.

Andrew Jackson died in 1845 of heart failure and dropsy. His efforts would be carried on by Martin Van Buren, his former secretary of state and vice president, who became president in 1837. According to historian Daniel Feller, we are told that Jackson was grateful to Martin Van Buren for his help in conducting foreign policy with France and Britain and his work in getting rid of the disloyal bureaucracy by replacing them with loyal Democrats.[38]

A political cartoon of President Andrew Jackson carrying Vice President Martin Van Buren into the White House.
https://commons.wikimedia.org/wiki/File:The_rejected_Minister.jpg

---

[38] "Andrew Jackson Leaves Office: Martin Van Buren Becomes President." (2014). *Voice of America Multimedia Site.* https://learningenglish.voanews.com/a/andrew-jackson-van-buren/1775693.html.

President Martin Van Buren continued to support and carry out the Indian Removal Act, praising his predecessor Andrew Jackson for his efforts at moving the Native Americans westward. In 1837, he called the displacement of Native Americans "a settled policy of the country" and said that it was for their well-being. In a message to Congress in 1838, Van Buren stated that "a mixed occupancy of the same territory by the white and red man is incompatible with the safety or happiness of either."[39]

In 1838, President Van Buren sent the army to expel the remaining Cherokee who had asked for more time to prepare. A few hundred Cherokee, without the authority or knowledge of tribal leaders, had signed the Treaty of New Echota in 1835, which stated the Cherokee would give up their lands and move west of the Mississippi within two years. John Ross, the principal chief of the Cherokees, had begged Congress to void the treaty, but his pleas fell on deaf ears. Almost all of the Cherokee were forced to move west.

---

[39] Landry, Alysa. "Martin Van Buren: The Force Behind the Trail of Tears." (2018). *ICT. An Independent Nonprofit News Enterprise.* https://indiancountrytoday.com/archive/martin-van-buren-the-force-behind-the-trail-of-tears.

Chapter 6: Attacking the Muscogee (Creek)

Following the many wars with the Native American tribes in the Southeast and the violation of numerous treaties by the US government, the refusal by the remaining Creeks in Alabama to relocate after their defeat at Horseshoe Bend angered President Andrew Jackson, making him determined to remove the remaining tribes west of the Mississippi. The Creeks had already been pushed out of Florida and Georgia, and now the stage was set for the remaining Creeks (Muscogee) to be removed from Mississippi and Alabama.

But before we get into Jackson's presidency and what they did with the Creek "problem," let's take a look at one of the most prominent Creek leaders. William McIntosh was born to a Scottish father and a Senoia mother and lived on the west bank of the Chattahoochee in Georgia. He taught himself English and blended in well with the settlers and the Creeks.[40]

William was known as Tustunnegge Hutker, or "White Warrior," for his participation in the War of 1812, during which time the Creek Nation split into the Lower Creek and the Upper

---

[40] Bullman, James A. "William, McIntosh Creek Indian (Muskogean)."
https://www.unknownscottishhistory.com/pdf/William_McIntosh_Creek_Indian_(Muskogean).pdf.

Creek. McIntosh became the leader of the Lower Creek in southern Georgia, while the Upper Creek resided in Georgia and Alabama. When the Red Sticks split from the Upper Creeks and demanded that the traditional leadership be maintained, the Creeks were effectively at war with each other. However, this war led to the settlers, the US government, and state militias getting involved.

As we said earlier, the settlers encroached on Native American lands, and the government troops and militias came to the aid of the settlers, burning Native American villages and massacring warriors, women, and children. They also enacted treaties that were constantly broken.

The Native Americans did not always take a peaceful diplomatic approach, especially since, to them, it seemed like it would have no effect. They also massacred women, children, and soldiers and burned settlements. These wars were bloody and fraught with tensions.

Chief McIntosh was one of the dissident natives who negotiated treaties with the US government, often doing so without the approval of the Creek National Council. In return, he received large sums of money and land for himself. His actions brought him into conflict with the Upper Creek tribes, who viewed him as a traitor who fraudulently gave away Creek territory that he had no right to give.

The first of the treaties McIntosh was involved in was the 1814 Treaty of Fort Jackson. This treaty was signed after the Red Stick Creek faction was defeated at the Battle of Horseshoe Bend. The terms of the treaty stated the Creek National Council had to cede twenty-three million acres of land in Alabama to the US government. The treaty put an end to the Creek War and saw the dissolution of the Red Sticks, who were forced to move with the rest of the Creeks.

Chief McIntosh fought on the side of the government more than once, including in the fight against the Seminoles. For signing the Treaty of Indian Springs in 1821, McIntosh received 1000 acres in Indian Springs, Georgia, and another 640 acres on the Ocmulgee River. When he signed the Treaty of Indian Springs in 1825, he gave away all the Creek land in Georgia and large parts of Alabama. The payment for this was $400,000, with McIntosh getting $200,000 and another $25,000 for his land at Indian Springs.[41]

For disobeying council law, Chief McIntosh was hunted down by his old enemy, Upper Creek Chief Menawa. In 1825, two hundred warriors set McIntosh's house on fire. He was pulled from the flames and was stabbed and shot to death. Other signees of the treaty were also targeted.

After the murder of Chief McIntosh, the leader of the Creek National Council, Opothle Yoholo, and a delegation of Upper Creeks traveled to Washington to appeal to "the Great White Chief," President John Quincy Adams. Opothle told the president the treaty had been signed without the people's consensus in mind. The president agreed with the Upper Creek delegation, saying the Treaty of Indian Springs should be made invalid.

A new treaty was established, the Treaty of Washington (1826), which gave all land east of the Chattahoochee River to the Creeks for a one-time payment of $217,600 and a yearly annuity of $20,000. It also provided funds for the Creeks to search for new lands west of the Mississippi and to relocate.

The governor of Georgia, George Troup, was angered at this turn of events and began to send surveyors to map out the lands ceded under the Treaty of Indian Springs. He also established a lottery for settlers to win allotments on the land in question. President Adams sent troops to enforce the Treaty of Washington. But when Troup called out the militia, Adams feared a civil war might break out. He backed down and allowed the Georgia legislature to renegotiate the settlement, with Troup seizing all the Creek lands on the borders of Georgia. By 1827, almost all of the Creeks were removed from Georgia, and several years later, many of the remaining Creeks would be removed from Alabama.[42]

The Treaty of Cusseta of 1832 divided Creek lands into allotments so they could either sell their allotments for money to move west or remain and obey state laws. Squatters didn't care what the treaties said and continued moving into Creek lands. By 1836, the Creeks had had enough. They rebelled against the land

---

[41] Ibid.
[42] "Trail of Tears: Creek Dissolution," (2002). https://www.liquisearch.com/trail_of_tears/creek_dissolution.

speculators and squatters and began the Second Creek War.

During this Creek uprising in Alabama, all the tensions between the land speculators, settlers, Native Americans, and the US government boiled over. As more and more Native American land was taken, various tribes began attacking and murdering white settlers. When President Jackson heard the news, he sent Francis Scott Key to assess the situation. Key reported that he found towns growing on Native American lands and documented numerous cases of fraud.[43]

The situation was out of control, with both sides committing heinous acts. President Jackson used the violence as justification to move the Creeks west. Some were bound in chains and marched to Montgomery, where they were then put on boats. Those Creeks who were seen as friendly were also forced to move.

---

[43] "The Creek War of 1836 in Alabama, Georgia, and Florida." https://exploresouthernhistory.com/secondcreekwar.html.

Chapter 7: The Original Death March? The Trail of Tears

Historian William Higginbotham, who says he did twenty years of research into government, military, and Cherokee records, claims that Gaston Litton, an archivist at the University of Oklahoma, said a Choctaw heard the phrase "Trail of Tears" used by another Choctaw who was speaking to a Baptist preacher. The phrase was about a road in Indian Territory, and after that, the term spread like wildfire. Higginbotham says the Native Americans in the mid-1800s never used the term and that it is a sleight-of-hand trick by cultural Marxists to slander Andrew Jackson. Such is revisionist historiography, which generally contradicts the gatekeeper's version of historical knowledge, but even if what Higginbotham says is true, the phrase can still apply to the plight of the Five Tribes as they moved west.[44]

It is true that an argument was made by government commissioners, settlers, politicians, and particularly President Andrew Jackson that it would be better to settle the Native Americans on new lands in the west for their safety and to prevent their annihilation by the settlers and the state militias. Higginbotham

---

[44] Higginbotham, William. "Trail of Tears, Death Toll Myths Dispelled." *The Oklahoman*, 1988. https://www.oklahoman.com/story/news/1988/02/28/trail-of-tears-death-toll-myths-dispelled/62660437007/.

said it was "to prevent their extinction given that many tribes in the north no longer existed." Another point where Higginbotham disagrees with the standard version of the Trail of Tears is the number that died. He argues that nowhere in the records is it recorded that four thousand Cherokee died on the way to Oklahoma; according to him, the number is probably somewhere between four hundred and eight hundred. He notes the Cherokee Nation files show that "the number of Indians departing the East ... is recorded at 12,623 the arrivals West at 12,783. Some stragglers joined on the way."

He also quotes T. Hartley Crawford as having said to the secretary of war in 1840 that the number was 447 and also notes that John Ross, the Cherokee chief, never talked about a large number of deaths on the march to Oklahoma, despite his many trips to Washington. We are also told that Ross's brother was the government supplier for the Native Americans en route to Indian Territory in Arkansas and Oklahoma. A doctor from the American Board of Commissioners for Foreign Missions named Elias Butler, a member of a Protestant group at Harvard, was sent to care for the sick. Supposedly, he was the one who spread the rumor of four thousand dead, which was only hearsay.

One other point revisionist historian Higginbotham makes is the notion of the Cherokee being "forced" to march. According to him, the idea of them marching at the end of bayonets through a cold winter to Oklahoma territory is incorrect. He makes the point that the Cherokee left their homelands of Georgia, Tennessee, and the Carolinas on their own after they requested more time from General Winfield Scott to prepare for the journey. Five thousand had voluntarily gone before them.

Higginbotham does not deny the Native Americans suffered but also states that Jackson and Van Buren were sympathetic to the Native Americans, as they supposedly believed that it would be better for the indigenous tribes to move westward.[45]

However, we must keep in mind that the move by the Five Civilized Tribes was at a much later date than, for example, the Delaware, who were forced westward to the Ohio Valley in the late

---

[45] Ibid.

1700s. The Cherokee were better prepared, having John Ross, an educated chief who spoke English, as their leader. Also, as Higginbotham reminds us, the Cherokee were initially paid $2.9 million for the relocation, which was later increased to $3 million by 1849 due to John Ross's persistence.

In the late 1700s, the Delaware were forced out of the northeast toward the Ohio River Valley, partly out of fear of the settlers' wrath and partly because they were getting caught up in the various American wars. They were given no funds to move, there were no doctors to accompany them, and there were no supply depots along the way. Historians tell us the Delaware, who lived in parts of New York and Pennsylvania, were led west by missionaries and guarded by US troops, which means they were effectively forced by violence and fraudulent treaties to leave their ancestral homes. Often, the chiefs signed the treaties with an "X," not understanding the ramifications of the document and hoping that a new homeland for their tribes lay ahead.

Revisionist history aside, the Trail of Tears is generally written as a tragic epoch in the history of America because it was one. Some compare it to the Bataan Death March, where the Japanese army marched American and Filipino prisoners approximately seventy miles to Camp O'Donnell, where thousands of Filipinos and hundreds of American soldiers died. Of course, the Native American displacement was on a grander scale. Many men, women, and children died of disease and starvation, while others froze to death or died of other causes along the long trek over land and water. The Trail of Tears is a network of various routes; altogether, they total up to be over five thousand miles.

In the 1830s, the Five Civilized Tribes—the Cherokee, the Choctaw, the Creek or Muscogee, the Chickasaw, and the Seminole—were targeted to move westward. According to Bruce Johansen in his article "Jacksonian Indian Policy," Jackson fought with and against the Native Americans and always intended to remove them from the Southeast, as proven by his refusal to acknowledge Supreme Court decisions in favor of Native American sovereignty. However, that does not prove he did not sympathize with them or that he did not believe they could rebuild and live a peaceful life in Oklahoma.[46]

Johansen says the Indian Removal Act marked a major shift in US relations with Native Americans, as the policy of "segregating Indians within states changed to moving Indians beyond the frontier—to pushing them from sight," thus setting Native Americans on a path of misery in their march west toward Oklahoma.

In his article, Johansen tells us the first of the Five Civilized Tribes to be forced to march on the Trail of Tears was the Choctaw in Mississippi, who were moved after they were tricked into signing the Treaty of Doak's Stand. They moved west onto lands that settlers already occupied, which were thirteen million acres in what is present-day Oklahoma.

Consequently, the treaty, which promised 640 acres of land to each household, with 320 acres to each child over ten, and each young child 120 acres, was not honored. And as usual, the government refused to intervene. The remaining six thousand Choctaw chose to remain in Alabama and Mississippi, where they were forced to accept the rule of the state governments in return for allotments of land. Finally, after three treaties had been violated, the Choctaw gave up all their lands east of the Mississippi, for which they received no recompense, and their relocation began in 1831. It took three years to complete, and it is estimated that 2,500 to 3,000 Choctaw died of starvation, disease, and exposure to the elements along the way.

---

[46] Johansen, Bruce. "Jacksonian Indian Policy, 1818-1832." https://americanindian2-abc-clio-com.ezproxy.liberty.edu/Search/Display/2219984.

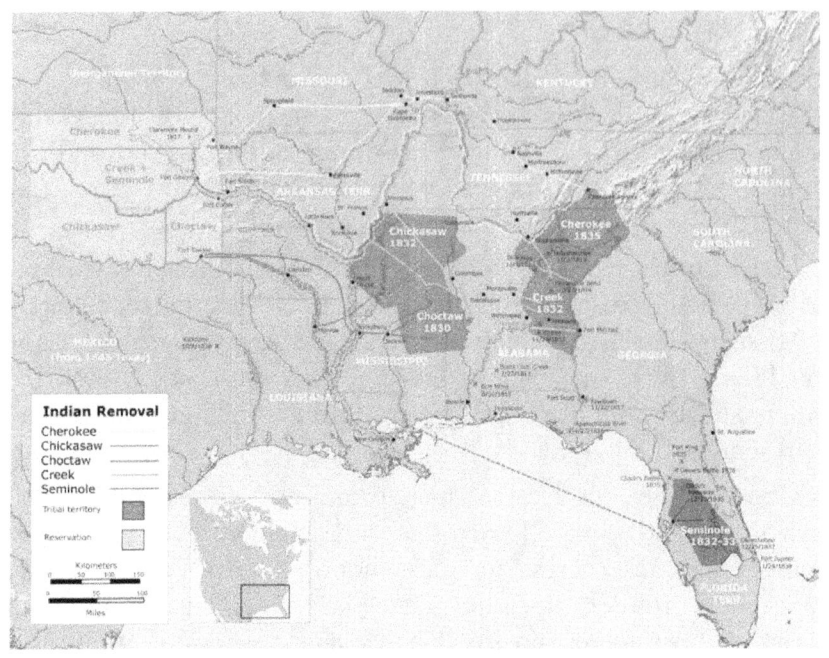

A map of the Trail of Tears.
https://commons.wikimedia.org/wiki/File:Trails_of_Tears_en.png

The Trail of Tears is more than just a trail; it is also a representation of the suffering and deaths the Native Americans experienced as they were displaced. Under pressure from Mississippi settlers who wanted the rich cotton lands the Native Americans occupied, President James Monroe attempted to push the Choctaw out of Mississippi in 1818, with Secretary of War John Calhoun arguing the tribe should decide without coercion. Ultimately, Andrew Jackson was sent to negotiate with the Choctaw, and when the talks failed, he angrily attacked Calhoun and the missionaries whom he said were blocking the removal. With the Choctaw refusing to relocate, claiming that land to the west of the Mississippi was unsuitable for farming, Jackson became more determined to force their removal.

Jackson tried again to force the Choctaw west of the Mississippi. In a second conference held in 1820, a treaty was signed by Chief Pushmataha, with the Choctaw agreeing to give up five million acres in exchange for land in Arkansas. But forcefully pushing the Choctaw west only made matters worse, especially since the settlers in Arkansas were already occupying the designated relocation lands.

With the election of Andrew Jackson to the presidency in 1828, the pressure to move the Native Americans out of Mississippi heated up. The arguments now centered around states' rights, an important factor in the legal battles the Choctaw, the Cherokee, and other tribes were waging in court.

The election of Jackson, who expressed his determination to relocate the Native Americans, emboldened government officials in Mississippi, who now felt they had the backing to dislodge the Choctaw from their ancestral lands. In the late 1820s, the state of Mississippi extended its civil and criminal laws over the Choctaw and Chickasaw, outlawing tribal governments. And with Jackson in power, the state government went even further. The Choctaw were threatened and coerced by the commissioners, who told them that whites would pour in and annihilate them if they did not agree to relocate to Arkansas.

Fearing for the safety of their people, tribal leaders in 1830 allowed a self-serving tribal chief named Greenwood LeFlore to negotiate a final removal treaty, in which LeFlore would be given land in Mississippi where he could build a cotton plantation. LeFlore would later go into hiding in fear for his life since many of the tribes did not want to relocate.

Subsequently, the other chiefs, jealous of LeFlore's influence with the commissioners, signed the Treaty of Dancing Rabbit Creek on September 27th, 1830, agreeing to give up the rest of their lands and move to western Arkansas. Under duress and with false promises by the government and the threat of attacks by the settlers, the Choctaw signed the treaty and gave away all their lands east of the Mississippi. As compensation, they were given a twenty-year annuity of twenty thousand dollars with which to build schools, churches, and a tribal council house in Indian Territory.

The harsh terms of the treaty stated that each family would receive one blanket when they reached the end of the trail, that the removal had to be made within three years, and that the families would be given small allotments of land. But the Indian commissioner ignored this last article, denying them the promised land allotments when they arrived. The infuriated tribe threatened an uprising, and LeFlore fled in fear. The US cavalry was again sent in to terrorize the Choctaw into submission.[47]

With the government controlling their annuity funds and government troops watching over them, the Choctaw had no choice in the matter of relocation. In November 1830, the Choctaw, having been led to believe they would be taken care of along the journey, had no idea of the suffering they would endure. For them, the Trail of Tears began in the fall of 1831, and the travel routes varied. Some started at Vicksburg by crossing the river, while others traveled by land to Memphis. Other people took steamboats down the Mississippi River and then up the Red River. Many took steamboats up to the relocation outpost, while others traveled on foot, horseback, or by wagon.

Of course, a frigid winter came, and many Choctaws froze to death along the way. There were no food provisions provided by the government, and if the accompanying commissioner did not buy food along the way, many people would have died of starvation. At the camps near Encore Fabre, Arkansas, there was no shelter and no food supplies, and the temperature was below zero. According to the diaries of the survivors, those who made it to this relocation marker fared a bit better than those who went south toward Louisiana, as many of those who went south got lost in the swamps and had to be rescued by boats. They then went from Monroe, Louisiana, to Arkansas, where they ventured onward to the Choctaw reservation.

Those who traveled to Memphis were afraid to board the boats headed to Arkansas because of a cholera epidemic and decided to travel overland through the Mississippi swamps, intending to cross the White River to Rock Roe, a bayou in Arkansas. While they were crossing the Grand Prairie to Little Rock, a cholera outbreak occurred in 1832, causing widespread deaths.

The surviving Choctaw finally reached the Choctaw Nation in present-day Oklahoma by 1833. The Choctaw experienced great suffering during their forced relocation. They were wracked by dysentery and cholera due to the lack of sanitary drinking water.

---

[47] DeRosier, Arthur H. "Andrew Jackson and the Negotiations for the Removal of the Choctaw Indians." *The Historian*, vol. 29, no. 3 (1967). https://www.jstor.org/stable/24442605.

They had gotten lost in the swamps, supplies were few and far between, thieves stole their horses and livestock, and whiskey purveyors preyed upon the desperate people. By 1836, fifteen thousand Choctaw had been relocated, and the few thousand who remained behind were being harassed. Many of them were forced to leave as well.

The Cherokee who lived in northern Georgia, Tennessee, and Alabama had been forcibly removed from their homelands since the 1820s. Their territory had been reduced by the influx of settlers and the various treaties that had been broken by the state and federal governments. Many voluntarily migrated westward, albeit under pressure.

As was the case with the Choctaw and Mississippi officials, the Georgia government was strengthened in its determination to expel all the Cherokee from the state. In 1828, Georgia took jurisdiction over Cherokee territory, and with the passing of the Indian Removal Act of 1830, it outlawed the Cherokee government, established the Georgia Guard, and took control of gold mines on Native American territory, forbidding them to mine for gold.

With the Cherokee leaders split over the issue of removal and the Cherokee National Council rejecting treaty after treaty, the Treaty of New Echota was signed in 1835 by the faction called the Treaty Party against the wishes of Chief John Ross's National Party. The treaty was negotiated by Indian Commissioner John Freeman Schermerhorn and non-elected officials of the Cherokee tribe. It stated the entire Cherokee Nation would be relocated west of the Mississippi River.

Expecting a harsh winter, the leaders asked for time to prepare. Some, like John Ross, went to Washington to find support and ask for the treaty to be nullified since it did not represent the majority of the tribe's desires. The government did not heed his request, and in the spring of 1838, General Winfield Scott arrived and began rounding up the Cherokee who remained behind. He placed them into camps in preparation for the trek toward modern-day Oklahoma.

The Cherokee faced the same harsh conditions as the Choctaw who marched before them. Water and food supplies were in short supply; measles, cholera, and dysentery outbreaks killed many; and the cold winters took their toll on the hapless Cherokee. Supply depots were set up along the way, and the caravan had a doctor accompanying them, but despite these preparations, the Cherokee suffered just as much as the other tribes in their westward trek.

The waterways in Arkansas were low due to the drought, so the Cherokee were unable to board boats. They were forced to walk, many doing so barefoot, to Dwight Mission, Oklahoma, in May 1834. By 1837, the last of the two antagonistic Cherokee parties, including John Ross and his family, arrived at Fort Coffee, meeting Jackson's deadline of 1838.[48]

However, fourteen thousand Cherokee were still in the Southeast by May 1838. Jackson ordered the state militias to round them up from the disease-ridden camps, where they had suffered in the summer heat. At Ross's Landing in Chattanooga, Tennessee, Lieutenant Edward Deas marched a group 120 miles to Decatur, Alabama, after which they went by rail to Tuscumbia. There, under heavy guard, they were loaded onto a steamboat. Most Cherokees had no possessions since they were forced out of their homes on short notice. After the kindly steamboat operator bought clothes for them, they headed for Fort Coffee in Oklahoma.

The next group of 875 was brought to Ross's Landing, but they were more resistant since they refused to give their names and refused the clothing offered to them. On the route to Lewisburg, Arkansas, hundreds escaped, but 722 arrived by August 1st. With low water levels in the south, steamboats could not be used, and the next party had to travel by road from Ross's Landing to Bellefonte, where hundreds escaped. Finally, they arrived at Waterloo, where a steamboat shipped them to Little Rock. By the time they arrived at the Cherokee Nation in September, 141 had died, and 293 had made their escape. Only three hundred actually made it to Arkansas.[49]

Another group of Cherokees, who also suffered illness and death along the way, were herded overland to Memphis and then once

---

[48] Littlefield, Daniel F. "Cherokee Removal." *The American Mosaic: The American Indian Experience*. https://americanindian2-abc-clio-com.ezproxy.liberty.edu/Search/Display/1595705.

[49] Ibid.

again overland to Little Rock, arriving in Indian Territory in the early months of 1839.

These remaining fourteen thousand Cherokee were better prepared for the hazardous journey simply because the removal was more organized by that point. The party had assistant conductors, wagon masters, teamsters, and doctors. Arrangements were also made for supplies to be given at certain points along the way. It is believed four thousand Cherokee perished along the way. The estimates are based on tribal and military records, so unlike what some revisionist historians think, the numbers are not pulled out of thin air.

Chapter 8: Legal Implications and Rebuilding the Cherokee Tribe

The legal implications of the displacement of Native Americans from their ancestral lands revolve around the idea that the Native American tribes had a "natural right" to live on the lands they occupied. There are three various arguments: the issue of Native American sovereignty, states' rights, and the power of the federal government in the making of treaties.

In 1802, the US government guaranteed the Cherokees all the land they occupied within Georgia's territory, provided the Cherokees consented.[50] But we must keep in mind that the encroachment of Native American lands began way before the Compact of 1802. With the arrival of Ponce de León and Hernando de Soto on the shores of Florida, the clash of civilizations began to take its toll on both sides. A tit-for-tat war between the Native Americans and the white settlers lasted for centuries and left the Southeast covered in blood.

---

[50] Casebeer, Kenneth M. "Subaltern Voices in the Trail of Tears: Cognition and Resistance of the Cherokee Nation to Removal in Building American Empire." *University of Miami School of Law.* https://repository.law.miami.edu/umrsjlr/vol4/iss1/2/.

Did the Native Americans have a sovereign right to their ancestral lands? It is a legal question that was argued in the US government's executive, legislative, and judicial branches, with tribal chiefs being coerced into signing treaties they did not understand. Many times, the treaties were fraudulent, either through unscrupulous land speculators who sold land that was already occupied, government tricksters, dissident Native Americans who claimed to represent the whole tribe, and chiefs who signed treaties in exchange for money and land. At times, the states ignored the rulings of the courts, and the president often refused to enforce the laws enacted by Congress that protected the rights of Native Americans. Therefore, the Compact of 1802 was null and void before it was even signed.

From then on, the Native Americans realized that after years of wheeling and dealing, with lands being ceded to the government and private trading companies, they were ceding too much land and being forced into debt. The Cherokee National Council in 1819 decided to make no further cessions of land. An interesting fact is the different views of land ownership. The Native Americans traditionally believed in communal ownership, with an individual family giving the land back to the tribe, thereby giving the tribe implied ownership over all the land. The whites, on the other hand, used "judicial and common law rules and institutions," which allowed them to manipulate treaties to their benefit.[51]

Often, the Native Americans could not afford lawyers, and with Georgia passing more and more laws, it became harder to fight the states that claimed sovereignty over their land. Georgia practiced a "legal strategy of removal by inconvenience and approved vigilantism; withdrawing criminal law protections ... prohibiting Cherokees from appearing in court ... and making it a crime for any white to enter Cherokee land, by refusing Cherokee gold claims while recognizing white claims within Cherokee territory."[52] Therefore, white missionaries, teachers, craftsmen, and printing presses were no longer allowed on Cherokee lands.

---

[51] Ibid.
[52] Ibid.

Hundreds of agreements were violated and broken in the 1700s and 1800s. The Cherokees' futile fight for justice continued until 1829 when the Cherokees filed a petition to Congress stating they did not agree to vacate their ancestral lands and demanded the government provide them with legal protection. However, with the election of Andrew Jackson in 1828, they had little hope of succeeding, especially when Jackson pushed through the Indian Removal Act of 1830.

It was around this time that the squabble began between Cherokee officials, with the anti-removal faction, led by John Ridge and Elias Boudinot, now realizing their struggle was hopeless. They began to think the only way to prevent the annihilation of the Cherokee Nation was to agree to resettlement in modern-day Oklahoma.

This brings us to the *Cherokee Nation v. Georgia* case of 1830, with Chief John Ross and Attorney William Wirt (the attorney general under John Adams's administration) arguing that the state of Georgia was making unconstitutional laws that, in effect, would "directly ... annihilate the Cherokees as a political society."[53] Georgia countered by arguing the Cherokee were claiming to be a foreign nation whose rights were being violated. In Georgia's eyes, the Cherokee could not claim the designation of a foreign country since they had no legitimate government. Ultimately, the court ruled the Cherokee Nation was not a foreign country. It was considered a "domestic dependent nation" by the framers of the Constitution and, therefore, had no grounds to bring forward a suit.

Chief Justice John Marshall stated the Cherokee Nation's relationship with the federal government was comparable to "a ward of the state," while Justice William Johnson wrote the "rules of nations" would see the Native Americans as "nothing more than wandering hordes." However, the dissenting justices, Smith Thompson and Joseph Story, wrote the Cherokee Nation had "usages, customs, and self-government" and was a government as designated by the Congressional Act of 1802. This meant the Supreme Court had jurisdiction over the case. The two justices

---

[53] "Cherokee Nation v. Georgia."
https://en.wikipedia.org/wiki/Cherokee_Nation_v._Georgia.

argued the Cherokee suit for injunction against the state of Georgia should be granted.[54]

One year after this case, in 1832, the legal challenge brought by Reverend Worchester against Georgia reached the Supreme Court. In this case, the Cherokee finally received what they perceived as a victory, with the court ruling they were a sovereign nation. Cherokee leader Elias Boudinot, a writer and newspaper editor, rejoiced, proclaiming Georgia's law was declared to be null and void by the highest judicial tribunal in the country. The Cherokees celebrated with rejoicing and dancing. However, the court decision did not prevent Georgia from keeping Reverend Worchester in jail (he refused to take a pardon so he could bring the case to the Supreme Court). Georgia also ignored the Supreme Court's ruling.[55]

The irony is that the federal government under President Jackson refused to intervene, claiming the state of Georgia was a sovereign entity, as proven by Justice Marshall's previous decision in *McCulloch v. Maryland*, where Marshall recognized the power of a state to preempt or forestall the actions of the federal government. In the case of *Worchester v. Georgia*, Jackson deferred to Marshall's decision, which he claimed limited his power regarding the state of Georgia, thereby giving Georgia tacit permission to continue its displacement of the Cherokees and setting a precedent for future nullification.

Regarding the decision in *Worcester v. Georgia* and Georgia's refusal to obey the Supreme Court, Andrew Jackson reportedly said to General John Coffee that "The decision of the Supreme Court has fallen stillborn, and they find that it cannot coerce Georgia to yield to the mandate."[56]

In summing up the legal battles of the Cherokee against the state of Georgia in 1831 and 1832, we can point to a passage in "Subaltern Voices in the Trail of Tears" ("subaltern" being the voices of the Native Americans crying out for help against an

---

[54] Ibid.

[55] Casebeer, Kenneth M. "Subaltern Voices in the Trail of Tears: Cognition and Resistance of the Cherokee Nation to Removal in Building American Empire." *University of Miami School of Law*. https://repository.law.miami.edu/umrsjlr/vol4/iss1/2/.

[56] Boulware, Tyler. "Cherokee Indians." *New Georgia Encyclopedia*, 20 January 2009, https://www.georgiaencyclopedia.org/articles/history-archaeology/cherokee-indians/.

imperialist giant):

"The States persecuted the Cherokees and asserted territorial control over the Nation, foreclosed a law strategy via state courts, forced the Law strategy into federal courts where the nation was denied sufficient vindication of sovereignty until too late to change the political deluge and denied enforcement of the federal law of treaties by the Constitution ... although the federal courts were open to protect the rights of American [white] citizens derived from Cherokee sovereignty."[57]

But despite everything the Cherokee suffered over a twenty-year period, they were able to rebuild their nation after arriving in Arkansas and Oklahoma. In the winter of 1838, John Ross and his wife, Elizabeth or "Quatie," who was seriously ill at the time, made their way west. She died on the *Victoria*, a steamboat that Ross had purchased for part of the journey, just before reaching Little Rock. She was buried in Little Rock Cemetery. Ross arrived in the early months of 1839, and the unification of the Western and Eastern Cherokee began. By September, they had ratified a constitution, built a courthouse, and established newspapers, schools, and businesses. Once the Civil War broke out, things changed drastically for everyone in the country, and the Cherokee Nation was no exception.

---

[57] Casebeer, Kenneth M. "Subaltern Voices in the Trail of Tears: Cognition and Resistance of the Cherokee Nation to Removal in Building American Empire." *University of Miami School of Law.* https://repository.law.miami.edu/umrsjlr/vol4/iss1/2/.

Chapter 9: Historical Legacy

While all the key decisions that led to the Trail of Tears and their outcomes could fill multiple books, there are a few that had a lasting impact on the American landscape, which at the time was rapidly expanding westward.

We can start by looking at the Spanish settlers who settled in the territory of modern-day Florida in the 1500s and how these explorers clashed with the Seminoles who occupied the territory. Ponce de León was killed when he returned to Florida in 1521 to search for the mythical Fountain of Youth, but he was followed by Hernando de Soto, who died of one of the diseases the settlers brought with them.[58]

We are told that smallpox, measles, malaria, and yellow fever killed over 90 percent of the Native Americans in North America, and this was, in a way, one of the causes of the Trail of Tears. Diseases wiped out settlements and entire tribes, leading to groups banding together or fighting against each other for more territory. Siding with the colonists ended up becoming essential in some cases because the Native Americans did not have the numbers to deal a decisive victory on their own. And with their decline in numbers, it became easier and easier for the white settlers to dictate decisions since they were the majority.

---

[58] "Collision of Worlds." https://www.semtribe.com/stof/history/CollisionofWorlds.

Spain finally ceded Florida to the US after signing the Adams-Onís Treaty of 1819. By this point, Andrew Jackson had already made incursions into the territory to stop the Seminoles from raiding settlers outside of Florida. Jackson was told to invade Florida to go after the Native Americans but to leave Spanish forts alone. The primary reason for the Seminole attacks on the Florida-Georgia border was retaliation for Southern militia coming into their territory to capture escaped slaves. The Seminoles also wanted to prevent settlers from stealing land and cattle.

The Southern states, particularly Georgia, put pressure on the US government, urging it to subdue the Seminole. And this was when Jackson entered the picture. The Treaty of Payne's Landing in 1832 urged the Seminoles to move west if they could find good land, but the scouts could not find livable territory. The treaty was signed, but many chiefs were bullied into doing it, so they continued to resist relocation. After the Adams-Onís Treaty, the US, which had full control of Florida, used the idea of Manifest Destiny to relocate the Seminoles. Ultimately, the decision was made to remove all the Seminoles from Florida, paving yet another path on the Trail of Tears.

In 1820, General Andrew Jackson and Thomas Hinds oversaw the Treaty of Doak's Stand, in which the Choctaw of Mississippi agreed to give up one-third of their land for a million acres in the west. The Choctaw removal began, and the point of no return was reached by the Native American tribes, who were losing the fight against the US government. Before this, one-fourth of the Cherokee Nation had voluntarily agreed to relocate to Arkansas territory, settling between the Arkansas and White Rivers. This intensified their struggle with the Osage, a struggle that had been going on since the 1760s when the Western Cherokee began moving to Osage territory.

In 1817, the Western Cherokee carried out a revenge attack on their traditional enemies, the Osage, massacring the village of Pasuga at Claremore Mound in present-day Rogers County, Oklahoma. The Osage were further incensed when they were forced to cede more territory under the Treaty of Fort Gibson in 1825, and their historical struggle with the Cherokee began once again after the passage of the Indian Removal Act in 1830 when the Eastern

Cherokee were forced to move west.

Another key decision that led to the Trail of Tears that is often overlooked was the Louisiana Purchase in 1803. Thomas Jefferson made a deal with France in which the US purchased over 800,000 square miles of land west of the Mississippi for fifteen million dollars. After the purchase, the gradual process of expelling Native Americans from Louisiana began in 1803, lasting until 1840. Jefferson's idea was for the Native Americans in Louisiana, including the Choctaw and the Natchez, to assimilate into European culture. If they resisted, they should be removed. But this was not to be since most were removed from Louisiana by treaties.

The Supreme Court rulings in the *Cherokee Nation v. Georgia* and *Worchester v. Georgia* led to important decisions involving the issue of federalism. The issue is a complicated one, but essentially, federalism or decentralization is the division of powers between the federal government and the state governments, with the Constitution as the arbiter.

To quickly recap the cases, the Supreme Court dismissed the first case brought by the Cherokee Nation, saying that it lacked merit because the Cherokee did not have the standing to claim sovereignty because it was not a foreign nation. In the second ruling (*Worchester v. Georgia*), the Supreme Court said because the Cherokee Nation had a government, it did have sovereignty. This decision angered the state of Georgia, which ignored the decision and continued to displace the Native Americans, with the president, Andrew Jackson, doing nothing to enforce the Supreme Court ruling.

These decisions caused the issue of slavery to flare up and rallied calls to abolish slavery. Andrew Jackson was a supporter of slavery (he owned slaves himself, as did the Cherokee and other Native Americans) and, thus, opposed the abolitionist movement. President Jackson had widespread support among Northern and Southern Democrats who supported slavery during his time as president, but the calm that ensued after the Missouri Compromise (1820) was now turning into a storm over slavery, mostly caused by Northern agitators spreading propaganda throughout the South.[59]

---

[59] Henig, Gerald S. "The Jacksonian Attitude Toward Abolitionism in the 1830s." *Tennessee*

The fires were again stoked when Mexico freed its slaves in 1829, frightening the slaveholders in Texas, which was still part of Mexico at the time, and by the publication of the *Liberator* by William Lloyd Garrison, a Northern abolitionist, in 1831. In the fall of that year, the Nat Turner rebellion in Virginia occurred. Sixty white citizens were massacred, inciting tensions between slaveholders and defenders of the institution and those who wished to either dismantle it or decrease its influence, especially in newly created states. The discussion over slavery led to arguments about states' rights and the possible dissolution of the Union. Jackson, a slaveowner and defender of states' rights, was at the time supported by his vice president, Martin Van Buren. Later, to maintain the support of Southerners, Van Buren stated in his 1837 Inaugural Address that "slavery must be left to the control of the slaveholding states themselves, without molestation or interference from any quarter."

Even the famous American writer James Fenimore Cooper, who wrote *The Last of the Mohicans*, supported President Jackson in his belief that states should regulate their own affairs, saying that "Congress did not have the power to interfere with slavery and that it rested entirely with the different states."[60]

So, we can see how the events of the early 1800s, the treaties with Native Americans, the court battles for Native American rights, and the displacement of the tribes to Oklahoma came to play a role in the future of America. States' rights and the power of Congress and the executive branch to control the states on certain issues were discussions that were held during the Native American removal. The people began to see that the states had more rights, and when that idea began to be infringed upon by the US regarding slavery, there were many people who were not happy.

Regarding the rise of the anti-removal movement, we are told by Mary Hershberger in her scholarly article titled "Mobilizing Women, Anticipating Abolition: The Struggle Against Indian Removal in the 1830s" that women across the country signed

---

Historical Quarterly, vol. 28, no. 1, 1969, pp. 42–56. *JSTOR*, http://www.jstor.org/stable/42623057.
[60] Ibid.

petitions defending the rights of Native Americans, saying that not only were they protected by previously signed treaties but also that they had become successful farmers and tradesmen. The first two prominent women opposing the Indian Removal Act were Catharine Beecher and her sister Harriet Ward Stowe (the future author of *Uncle Tom's Cabin*), who launched a petition drive in which many Americans protested the Indian Removal Act.[61]

Hershberger states that President Van Buren was stunned by the power of the anti-removal forces. The outcry and surge of petitions exasperated him, but he was determined to carry out Jackson's removal policy because Jackson had previously said that "no other subject was of greater importance than this." Hershberger argues that "the heart of Indian land policy had always been nothing less than land cessions to white markets, and treaties were the preferred weapon," ignoring the possibility of civil war if Jackson or Van Buren had used military force to remove white squatters from Native American lands.[62]

As we noted earlier, Jackson was being hammered by all sides, and Hershberger lays out in her critique the quandary that Jackson was in by stating the two rationales Jackson offered for removal. Firstly, "having an independent Indians nation residing within the borders of any state was an intolerable situation. And second, "that for their survival, southeastern Indians had to move across the Mississippi away from white encroachment."[63] The question of Jackson's sincerity is comparable to asking why Winston Churchill, a staunch anti-communist, suddenly embraced Joseph Stalin in WWII.

As we said earlier, in Jackson's Inaugural Address, he opposed Native American removal but began to embrace the idea in his first year of office. Were these his thoughts from his early days as a fighter against Native Americans? It's impossible to say, but the fact is that he pushed the Indian Removal Act of 1830 over the

---

[61] Hershberger, Mary. "Mobilizing Women, Anticipating Abolition: The Struggle against Indian Removal in the 1830s." *The Journal of American History*, vol. 86, no. 1, 1999, pp. 15–40. *JSTOR*, https://www.jstor.org/stable/2567405. Accessed 7 Oct. 2022.

[62] Ibid.

[63] Ibid.

objections of religious organizations and missionary outposts around the country.

The voluntary women's associations teamed up with religious institutions and their missionaries. A flurry of petitions was sent to Congress. As Hershberger tells us, the anti-removal movement merged with the abolitionist movement, with many activists realizing that removing Native Americans would be akin to removing blacks to Africa. Thus, the colonization movement became the abolitionist movement, and women's auxiliary organizations, together with the missionaries, took up the fight against Jackson's and Van Buren's Indian Removal Act.

Hershberger tells us that women who had no standing adopted a feeling of "Republican motherhood," using petitions in defense of widow's pensions, employment for the needy, and what they considered to be the inhumane act of Native American removal. They became, in effect, "the moral guardians of the nation's virtue," with one of their priorities being the establishment of Native American schools in the Northeast and the South. They did this by funding religious organizations and missionaries who established schools. One of the first missionary commissions was given to Charles Finney by the Utica Female Missionary Society in 1824.[64]

The denominational periodicals countered the arguments of critics who said the Native Americans were facing "extinction" by pointing to the numerous Cherokee schools and teachers, their commerce, and their widespread agriculture. The periodicals further argued the shame of the nation could be seen in the numerous massacres committed by white citizens, with several of them pointing to the 1782 massacre of over ninety Moravians in the village of Gnadenhutten in Ohio by a mob of whites. All the harsh acts carried out against the Native Americans were being published in these nationwide periodicals, and Jackson's election caused a spike in protests and an outpouring of sympathy for the Native Americans in these publications.

In 1829, the American Board of Commissioners for Foreign Missions led by Jeremiah Evarts printed the "William Penn Essays" in the *National Intelligencer*, outlining the treaties between the

---

[64] Ibid.

Native Americans and the US government and claiming that the Native Americans legally owned their land.

These essays were published around the country, even in the *Cherokee Phoenix*. Joyous sentiments were expressed by *The Journal of Commerce* and *the Christian Watchman*, saying the entire nation should "notice the feeling which is now excited in the community about the rights of the Aborigines of this country." Hershberger's research tells us the "William Penn Essays" were more popular than Thomas Paine's *Common Sense* and led to the two famous Supreme Courts cases of Cherokee *Nation v. Georgia* and *Worcester v. Georgia* and the rise of the women's movement that tied the anti-removal movement to the developing abolitionist movement. But despite these efforts, the Indian Removal Act passed, and the Supreme Court ruling in favor of Native American sovereignty was ignored by Georgia, with President Jackson turning a blind eye.[65]

Later, in 1837, the Pinckney Gag rule passed by Congress was designed to table anti-slavery petitions and stated that Congress had no right to interfere with slavery. Hershberger tells us that Catharine Beecher, who did her best to remain anonymous during the campaign, had a breakdown over the stress involved in petitioning and ultimately gave up the fight. She went into mainstream politics.

Thus, the events that occurred before and during the Jackson and Van Buren presidencies led to the virtual disappearance of the back to Africa movement (colonialist movement), which evolved into the nullification crisis of 1832 and the abolitionist movement, which as Henig states, "was one of the major ingredients prompting the transition of South Carolina from extreme nationalism in 1816 to extreme sectionalism in 1836."[66] Hence, we can see how the events that occurred in history between 1830 and 1850 led to a bloody civil war over the issues of tariffs placed on cotton (states' rights) and the anti-slavery movement (which stemmed from the anti-removal movement).

---

[65] Ibid.

[66] Henig, Gerald S. "The Jacksonian Attitude Toward Abolitionism in the 1830s." *Tennessee Historical Quarterly*, vol. 28, no. 1, 1969, pp. 42–56. *JSTOR*, http://www.jstor.org/stable/42623057.

And with the Civil War, history witnessed the North's victory, which put an end to the Confederacy and brought about the abolition of enslaved people. No one can argue that the Civil War did not alter the course of American history, as it brought about the Thirteenth, Fourteenth, and Fifteenth amendments to the US Constitution.

So, we can see how events that occurred a few hundred years ago shaped the legal, social, economic, and political landscape of America, which would eventually become an economic powerhouse in the world. As was noted earlier, the Native Americans did not fare too well in their quest for sovereignty, as their legal battles were stymied at every point, while the slaves were only fully freed at the end of the Civil War. Both groups of people still had to fight for their rights after the bloodshed stopped.

Chapter 10: Legendary Figures

Many important figures appeared during our journey through this time in American history, but in the looking glass, a few stand out.

"Mad" Anthony Wayne

When we read about George Washington and his struggle with Native American policies, historians tell us that he often sent General "Mad" Anthony Wayne to quell the disturbances. Mad Anthony, whose prominence stands out for his performance in the Revolutionary War, fought alongside General Washington and Marquis de Lafayette. General Wayne got his nickname when one of his spies was arrested for disorderly conduct in a small town. The general ordered that the lad be given twenty-nine lashes, and thereafter, the men called the general "Mad Anthony."[67]

When summoned by Washington to put down the Northwest Indian War, Wayne took a year to train his troops, which he called the Legion of the United States, and marched up to western Ohio to defeat Blue Jacket, the Shawnee war chief, in the Battle of Fallen Timbers in 1794. He then went on to negotiate the Treaty of Greenville (1795), which ended all tribal claims to Ohio and the surrounding areas.

---

[67] Hickman, Kennedy. "American Revolution: Major General Anthony Wayne." ThoughtCo, Aug. 28, 2020, https://thoughtco.com/major-general-anthony-wayne-2360619.

President Washington believed the Native Americans could be civilized, but that if that turned out not to be possible, bloodshed would be necessary. The next president, John Adams, felt that Native American removal should be voluntary, but over time, he supported thirty treaties that required Native Americans to give up the titles to their lands.

Thomas Jefferson

If we move on to the thinking of the third president, Thomas Jefferson, we can gain a deeper understanding of what shaped his thinking about the Native American "problem."

In Andrea Petrini's essay, "The Enlightenment of Thomas Jefferson," we are told Jefferson was schooled in the philosophy of the European Enlightenment, which meant he believed "the laws of human society and the physical world [can] be discerned through the scientific method." Quoting the American scholar Joseph Blau, he wrote that Jefferson believed that "open eyes and an active mind—enlightenment—were available to every man and were the guarantees of a good life." Jefferson later applied these thoughts to the American Revolution, believing that Americans should be free from the whims of the king of England and be able to express their natural rights in a "truly democratic society."[68]

Following the American Revolution, Jefferson began to theoretically apply these thoughts to the Native Americans, believing they could become civilized if they only agreed to change their ways, in effect becoming part of European-American society. Unlike Alexander Hamilton, Benjamin Franklin, and others before him, Jefferson never came to believe that blacks could be "equals of whites" but was ambivalent in his thinking regarding Native Americans, whom he believed were higher on the scale of races than African Americans. He even approved the marriages of his daughters to men who claimed to be distant relatives of Pocahontas. While Jefferson never allowed Native Americans to rise to the level of the white man, he began to believe they could be educated, especially when archaeologists in Ohio began uncovering Native American mounds and other designs with squares and circles, as

---

[68] Petrini, Andrea R. "The Enlightenment of Thomas Jefferson." https://elonuniversity.contentdm.oclc.org/digital/collection/p15446coll2/id/11/.

Jefferson had a lifelong fascination with geometry.[69]

Other evidence of his respect for Native Americans can be found in his book, *Notes of the State of Virginia*, where he laments the murder of Mingo Chief Logan's family by white settlers.[70] Jefferson admired Logan's speech to Lord Dunmore in which he said he would never surrender and "cited Logan's eloquence as proof of the verbal sophistication of a people without letters."[71] And while Jefferson spoke of Native Americans in the manner of "remarkable children" and never had a Native American friend, he still, nevertheless, believed they held an "intermediate" level above the race of blacks" though were still "in reason much inferior to whites" and incapable "of tracing and comprehending the investigations of Euclid."[72]

By studying Thomas Jefferson's thoughts on the question of Native American removal, in which he was involved only theoretically, we are given another view of what was going on in the decades before the Indian Removal Act of 1830. Jefferson's "civilization program" was based on making treaties by which he hoped the Native Americans would sell land to make room for white settlers while hoping the treaties would make them loyal to the United States and not to France or Britain.

Jefferson's hope was that the Native Americans would sell their lands, freeing up their hunting grounds on which white settlers could build homes. With their lands gone, it would push them further into debt, forcing them to sell more lands. In a somewhat contradictory letter to William Henry Harrison regarding the Louisiana Purchase, Jefferson encouraged selling goods to natives on a credit plan, hoping to satisfy the white settlers while stimulating the enlightenment of the Native Americans. It is unknown how putting them into debt would be helpful; it seems a dubious form of trickery that was also implicit in many of the treaties.

---

[69] Kennedy, Roger. "Jefferson and the Indians." *The University of Chicago Press, Vol. 27, No. 2/3.* (1992). https://www.jstor.org/stable/1181368.

[70] Jefferson, Thomas. *Notes on the State of Virginia.* University of North Carolina, 1982 (originally published in 1785).
https://www.jstor.org/stable/10.5149/9780807899809_jefferson.

[71] Kennedy, Roger. "Jefferson and the Indians."

[72] Ibid.

Still, Jefferson hoped the "enlightened" Native Americans could become peaceful farmers who would assimilate into white society. But again, we are reminded of the overwhelming number of white emigrants from Europe and the frantic push westward that eventually overwhelmed Jefferson's "civilization program" and the supposed "enlightenment" of the Native American tribes. These problems would only grow worse, bewildering and plaguing President William Henry Harrison and those who followed him.

Elias Boudinot

Elias Boudinot.
https://commons.wikimedia.org/wiki/File:Elias_Boudinot_(1802%E2%80%931839).jpg

Elias Boudinot was a Cherokee born in Oothcaloga, Cherokee Nation, in Calhoun, Georgia, in 1802. His birthname was Gallegina Watie, but he was known as Buck Watie before changing his name. After completing his studies at a local Moravian missionary school, Boudinot was sent to Cornwall, Connecticut, to observe a meeting of the American Board of Commissioners for Foreign Missions, where the goal was to train missionaries to spread Christianity and European culture to young Native American men.

By 1820, he had converted to Christianity after being inspired by his meeting with a New Jersey congressman named Elias Boudinot, who was also the president of the American Bible Society. The young Native American was so impressed by Elias Boudinot that he adopted his name. In 1824, the young Boudinot helped to translate the New Testament into Cherokee by using the system of symbols developed by a knowledgeable man named Sequoyah, a learned Cherokee who studied for twelve years and finally developed the Cherokee language in 1821.

Even though Boudinot lived in a time of racial prejudice, he married a white woman, after which they were burned in effigy. They were forced to return to New Echota.

In 1828, Boudinot published the first Native American newspaper, the *Cherokee Phoenix*, which used the syllabary Cherokee language developed by Sequoyah. He wrote many articles that were against Native American removal. He did write in favor of acculturation, which makes sense given his conversion to Christianity and schooling.

With the Indian Removal Act of 1830, Boudinot changed his views from acculturation and began to write in favor of Native American removal, going as far as to attack Cherokee Chief John Ross, who opposed the relocation of the Cherokees. Boudinot's views brought him into conflict with most of the tribe, as many resisted the idea of moving west of the Mississippi River. Boudinot believed that removal was inevitable. It was clear to him that Jackson would not back down, so it would be better for the Cherokee to secure the best terms for themselves.

In 1835, Boudinot and others signed the Treaty of New Echota, which stated that all Cherokees would relocate to Oklahoma. As we have talked about above, this treaty was not signed with the approval of Chief John Ross. In fact, most Cherokees disagreed with the treaty.

Before Boudinot could move west, he was stabbed to death outside his home. He was not the only one to be targeted. His cousin, John Ridge, and his uncle, Major Ridge, were seen as traitors to the Cherokee Nation. They were all killed on the same day; it is not known who authorized the murders. Boudinot's younger brother, Stand Watie, was also attacked but survived. He believed John Ross was behind it, but Ross claimed to have no part. Stand Watie went on to become a Confederate general. In 1959, Boudinot was inducted into the Georgia Newspaper Hall of Fame.

Chief John Ross

A photograph of Chief John Ross.
https://commons.wikimedia.org/wiki/File:John_Ross_of_the_Cherokee.jpg

John Ross, principal chief of the Cherokee tribe from 1828 to 1866, shepherded the Cherokee, helped them in their legal battles against the authorities, and guided them west to Oklahoma.[73] Born to a Cherokee mother and possibly a Scottish father, Ross learned about Cherokee culture from his grandmother and mother. He later fought with the US Army against the Red Sticks (a faction of the Creeks) after the massacre at Fort Mims, Alabama.

---

[73] Watts, Jennifer. "John Ross: Principal Chief of the Cherokee People." https://tnmuseum.org/junior-curators/posts/john-ross-principal-chief-of-the-cherokee-people?locale=en_us.

In the following years, Ross helped the Cherokee form a council, traveled to Washington to argue against the persecution and removal of the Cherokee, and helped to build a new Cherokee capital called New Echota in Gordon County in northwest Georgia.

In 1828, Ross was elected the principal chief of the Cherokee. He later assisted Quartermaster Sidney Jesup in negotiating with the Seminoles in Florida and subsequently went on to oppose the Treaty of New Echota in 1835.

After losing the battle to overturn the treaty, the remaining Cherokees began the long journey to Oklahoma in 1838 under the direction of General Winfield Scott. When they arrived in Oklahoma, John Ross assisted in the building of a new capital called Tahlequah, along with many public buildings and schools.

Osceola

Osceola.
https://commons.wikimedia.org/wiki/File:George_Catlin_-_Os-ce-o-l%C3%A1,_The_Black_Drink,_a_Warrior_of_Great_Distinction_-_1985.66.301_-_Smithsonian_American_Art_Museum.jpg

Osceola was a Seminole leader born in Georgia in 1804. He fought in the Second Seminole War in 1835 when General Andrew Jackson was sent in to capture the tribes and forcibly remove them from Florida to the west. He opposed the Treaty of Payne's Landing (1832), as he did not agree with those tribesmen who wanted to emigrate from Florida. In his anger, he murdered Chief Charley Emathla, who had agreed to the treaty, and US Indian Agent Wiley Thompson. Osceola was upset with Thompson's treatment of him. Thompson arrested Osceola for being disagreeable, and to secure his release, Osceola had to sign the Treaty of Payne's Landing.

For the next few years, Osceola and his warriors moved farther and farther into the swamps, eluding US troops and using guerilla tactics and surprise attacks to deal decisive blows on the American soldiers. Finally, in 1837, he and his followers were summoned under a flag of truce to Fort Peyton near St. Augustine to meet General Sidney Jesup. However, it was a trap. Osceola was captured, although most of the others were able to escape into the swamps.

John Horse

John Horse was a Seminole sub-chief. He was an African American Seminole of Spanish descent. To many, John Horse was a brave warrior. He had previously served as an officer in the Mexican army, where he defended free black settlements, and he later fought with Osceola against the US Army in Florida. He fought in the Second Seminole War and worked closely with Coacoochee.

Coacoochee

Coacoochee, also known as Wild Cat, was another important Seminole chief. Besides fighting in the Second Seminole War, he was respected as a high-ranking Seminole and thus held many offices in the Seminole community before and after the war.

After years of hiding in the swamps and carrying out guerilla attacks on American soldiers, he met with William Tecumseh Sherman near Fort Pierce in 1841. By this point, Osceola had died, and Coacoochee's father had also died while traveling westward. Coacoochee agreed to be taken to Fort Gibson in Oklahoma.

However, Coacoochee was not content with life on the reservation. He left in 1849, meeting up with John Horse. The two spent the next few years with a Kickapoo tribe and defended the Mexican border from American and hostile Native Americans. While acting as a supposed peacemaker between various tribes, he traveled between Mexico and Texas while secretly trying to build a Native American confederation. In 1857, he died in a smallpox epidemic in Mexico.

Micanopy

Micanopy was another Seminole chief who fought alongside Osceola, Holata Micco (Billy Bowlegs), and Coacoochee (Wild Cat), known as Gato del Monte by the Mexicans.

Micanopy was born around 1780 near St. Augustine, Florida, and he was known as the "Chief of Chiefs," although he wouldn't become principal chief until he was nearly forty years old.

Like other high-ranking Seminoles, he employed former slaves to tend his lands. It is believed Micanopy had over one hundred fugitive slaves in his employment. And like other Seminoles, Micanopy did not see blacks as being lesser. He even encouraged intermarriage between Seminoles and African Americans.

Micanopy supported Osceola in rebuking the Treaty of Payne's Landing and led warriors who annihilated General Francis Dade and his troops when they pursued him into the swamps. The Dade massacre kicked off the Second Seminole War.

In 1837, Micanopy was believed to be meeting with General Thomas Jesup under a flag of truce, but Jesup betrayed and captured him, along with Osceola. He was imprisoned in Charleston, South Carolina, and died soon after he was deported to Indian Territory. He died at Fort Gibson in 1849.

Seminole Chief John Jumper (Heneha Mekko)

A photograph of John Jumper.
https://commons.wikimedia.org/wiki/File:John_Jumper.jpg

John Jumper was the nephew of Micanopy. He was a Baptist minister and became a Seminole chief in 1849. Since the Seminoles had a matrilineal kinship system, after Micanopy passed, the position of chief went to his sister's children, first James (Jim) Jumper and then John. Before this happened, John Jumper fought in the Second Seminole War, leading two hundred warriors against the over one hundred soldiers led by US Army Major Francis Dade, who was sent into the swamps to capture the Seminoles. Dade's troops fell into the trap set by Jumper. Dade and his men were forty miles short of their intended destination of Fort King. Most of them fell in the battle.

Historian Frank Laumer says the Seminoles "made a terrible mistake by attacking the US Army in broad daylight." He further says that it "was an affront that simply could not be born according to the honor system of the time." This insult to the US Army made them more determined to capture the remaining Seminoles. Laumer believes that if this slaughter had not taken place, the Seminoles might have remained on their lands in Florida, as it was a place that nobody wanted. He writes about Florida, saying it was "a pestilential place, full of alligators and Indians. People termed it the most miserable place they ever saw."[74]

John Jumper was eventually captured. He was sent to Indian Territory but was later returned to Florida to convince the remaining Seminoles to relocate to Oklahoma. However, he was not successful, as the remaining Seminoles moved farther into the Everglades.

In 1861, John Jumper made an alliance between the Seminoles and the Confederate States of America. He was given the rank of major and later lieutenant colonel. After the war, he became a Baptist minister. He died at his home near Wewoka, Oklahoma, in 1896.

Abraham

Abraham was a slave born at the end of the 1700s in either Georgia or Florida, and he worked for a physician named Doctor Sierra in northern Florida. His opportunity for freedom arose when a British officer promised freedom to slaves who volunteered to fight with the British in the War of 1812 against the Americans.

By 1814, Abraham was laboring in a construction fort at Prospect Bluff, a British fort that would soon become a place of refuge for escaped slaves from the Carolinas and Georgia. Having spent his life in the wilds of Florida, Abraham had become acculturated with the Seminole people and found a common cause in their struggle for freedom against the US government.

Abraham quickly became a leader and quickly adapted to the customs and language of the Seminoles. Within a short time, he was considered a warrior, and they called him Suwanee Warrior for his defense of a town with the same name.

---

[74] Warren, Michael. "Dade's Massacre Reenacts Start of Second Seminole War." https://floridatraveler.com/dades-massacre-recalls-seminole-history/.

Back in 1813, he founded the Black Seminole town of Pilaklikaha, also known as Abraham's Town, where he was accepted as a member of the Seminole Nation. Prior to the First Seminole War (1817-1818), Abraham was living at Fort Prospect, also known as Negro Fort, on the Apalachicola River with three hundred escaped slaves and Red Sticks who had fled south from General Andrew Jackson's advances. When the Seminole settlements along the Apalachicola River were seen as a threat by the Southern planters, Jackson ordered the fort to be destroyed. The survivors, which included Abraham, escaped to the British post at Prospect Bluff.

In 1815, Major Edward Nicholls, the Irish major in charge, left for England, leaving the surviving Red Stick warriors and the escaped slaves with most of the ammunition and artillery. A black man named Garcon (some say he was a chief) commanded the fort with an unnamed Choctaw chief. They invited runaway slaves to settle in the fort, which offered protection. Soon, their settlement stretched fifty miles. General Andrew Jackson was worried the fort would only continue to grow, which would make it nearly impossible to tear down.

In July 1816, Jackson's forces and slave-hunting Creeks sailed to the fort. On July 27th, a gunboat shell landed in the ammunition depot of the fort and caught the magazine on fire, creating an explosion. Over three hundred people died, and almost everyone else inside the fort was injured. It is important to note that not everyone inside the fort was a soldier. Women and children were also killed.

The survivors, which included Abraham escaped. The Creeks captured Garcon and shot him. They scalped the Choctaw chief and stabbed him to death. The surviving slaves who weren't able to escape in the aftermath were returned to their owners.

Later in the Second Seminole War (1835-1842), Abraham served as a scout and an interpreter for Chief Micanopy. Not much is known about Abraham's death, but we do know that he later lived in Bowlegs Town on the Suwannee River and later married the widow of Billy Bowlegs.

General Thomas Sidney Jesup

The Seminoles were the last Native American tribe to be forcibly removed from their lands in Florida. Despite embarking on many campaigns, Andrew Jackson failed to dislodge the Seminoles. In 1836, he appointed Quartermaster Thomas Sidney Jesup, whom he considered a man of action, to deal with the remaining Creeks in Alabama and Georgia. He was later tasked with removing the remaining Seminoles, including the Black Seminoles, the escaped slaves who had joined the Seminole Nation, from Florida.

Jesup was born in the frontier county of Berkeley, Virginia, in 1788. His father, Major James Edward Jesup, was a decorated officer in the Revolutionary War. He married an Irish woman named Ann O'Neill, the sister of Colonel George Croghan, a man who received honors for his actions in the War of 1812 when he defended Fort Stephenson.

Nineteen-year-old Jesup joined the army in 1808 and was soon awarded the honor of being a second lieutenant, even though he had no experience. Due to his diligence as an officer, he was quickly promoted to first lieutenant. The fact that he grew up in a military family and lived on the frontier surrounded by hostile Native Americans gave him insight into what the army was doing wrong in its struggle with the native tribes.

In 1818, he was appointed brigadier general and quartermaster and began making plans for forts and outposts. He also found ways to better improve the conditions and morale of his troops. During the Second Seminole War, he was given command of US troops in Florida, which aligned with state militias and friendly Creeks. They had orders to move the Seminoles west of the Mississippi River.

Jesup saw the fugitive slaves as the key to capturing Seminole Chief Osceola, the Black Seminole leader John Horse, Micanopy and his black advisor and interpreter Abraham, Alligator, and Coacoochee. Jesup knew the Seminoles had a great love for the blacks who became part of the tribe. Most enslaved people became successful farmers; their only restriction was that they had to pay an annual tribute of part of their harvest to the Seminoles. Jesup felt that by disrupting the Seminole economy, he could force them to surrender. In a letter, he wrote, "This, you may be assured, is a negro problem, not an Indian war; and if it is not speedily put down, the south will feel the effects of it on their slave population before the end of the next season."[75]

General Jesup.
https://commons.wikimedia.org/wiki/File:Thomas_Sidney_Jesup.jpg

In November 1836, President Jackson appointed Thomas Sidney Jesup to command the American forces in Florida. He was the mediator with the War Department during the Second Seminole War. Jesup's orders were to clear the Native Americans from the banks of the Withlacoochee River in Florida and away from Fort King and Volusia near the St. Johns River.

But the elusive Seminoles slipped away into the swamps as the troops approached. The only thing Jesup accomplished in his first attack was capturing a village at the Hatchee-Lustee Creek, which was filled with women and children who had been left behind by the retreating Seminoles.

---

[75] "General Jesup." http://johnhorse.com/trail/02/c/01.htm .

Jesup's next attempt to capture the Seminole chiefs and their warriors, which numbered about four thousand, was in 1835 after Osceola attacked Fort King to kill his hated enemy, Indian Agent Wiley Thompson. Around the same time, his advisor, Micanopy, carried out the Dade massacre, in which Major Dade was attacked by around two hundred warriors. It is said Micanopy's first shot killed Dade, and a little over one hundred US soldiers were killed. Three soldiers survived, although one died of his wounds the next day.

In 1837, Jesup committed what was viewed as an act of treachery against the Seminoles. Under a false flag of truce, he summoned several chiefs to St. Augustine and managed to capture Osceola and Micanopy, although Coacoochee (Wild Cat) and other chiefs escaped. Even back then, this act was seen as cowardly and treacherous, lending support to the Seminole cause.

After failing to subdue the Seminoles, Jesup was wounded in battle in 1838 and was forced to retire, leaving General Zachary Taylor to carry on the fight.

Major Francis L. Dade

Major Francis Dade was born in Virginia in either 1792 or 1793. While not much is known about his childhood, we do know that at some point he joined the army and fought in the War of 1812. He was given command of the Fourth Infantry Unit in 1815 at the beginning of the Second Seminole War. He carried out military campaigns in the swamps between Fort Brooke in Tampa and Fort King in Ocala in 1825 and 1826, pursuing the elusive Seminoles, who were determined to resist relocation.

In 1828, Dade was promoted to major after serving as captain for ten years. When the Seminoles again carried out an uprising, he was ordered to leave his base at Key West and march to Fort Brooke, leading over one hundred soldiers on a campaign through the wilderness to capture the Seminoles who were led by Osceola and Micanopy.

Since the Seminoles had destroyed the bridges, Dade and his men were forced to wade through the swamps, where they were bogged down. The Seminoles set up an ambush on higher ground. They hid behind palmettos and other plants and trees and opened fire on the passing troops.

Major Dade was supposedly killed by Micanopy. Out of over one hundred soldiers, only three survived, although one later died of his wounds. The massacre was the brainchild of the Seminole, who had set the trap by destroying outposts, supply lines, and plantations throughout 1835.

Zachary Taylor

A photograph of Zachary Taylor.
https://commons.wikimedia.org/wiki/File:Zachary_Taylor_restored_and_cropped.jpg

Zachary Taylor, the twelfth president of the United States, was born into a wealthy plantation-owning family in Virginia in 1784 and spent his childhood in Kentucky. He later joined the army and was made a first lieutenant in 1808. He bought a plantation in Louisville, Kentucky, where he owned over two hundred slaves. However, he had little interest in growing cotton and was more interested in guarding the borders against Native American infiltration.

Taylor spent close to forty years in the military, and most of that time was spent fighting Native Americans. He fought in the Mexican-American War to acquire territory for slaveholders and became a hero after his victories at Buena Vista and Monterrey, paving the road for a possible attack on Mexico City. He fought the Shawnee in the War of 1812, fought the resistant Blackhawks in 1832, and in the Second Seminole War in 1837. In the Second Seminole War, he used bloodhounds to track the Seminoles who hid in the swamps. In an 1838 letter, he stated, "I am in favor of [using dogs] ... as the only means of ridding the country of the Indians ... who take shelter in swamps and hommocks ... only to ascertain where they are, not to worry them."

In December 1837, General Taylor, along with eight hundred regular soldiers, two hundred volunteers, and fifty Delaware warriors, fought the Battle of Lake Okeechobee, the largest and bloodiest battle of the Second Seminole War. They went up against approximately four hundred Seminole and Miccosukee on the northern shore of the lake.

General Taylor ignored the advice of his officers and used the same failed tactics that General Robert E. Lee would use at Gettysburg. Taylor employed a classic European frontal assault, hoping to win with a knockout blow. But the warriors hiding in the woods surprised the army as they waded through the muddy swamp. After the battle was all said and done, over twenty-five soldiers had been killed, and over one hundred were wounded. Around twelve Native Americans were found dead, with the rest escaping farther into the wetlands.

Both sides claimed victory, although the Seminoles won the tactical victory. General Zachery Taylor was declared a hero and was promoted to brigadier general. In 1849, Taylor became president.

At the end of the Second Seminole War, an estimated forty million dollars had been spent by the US government, although the actual cost might never be known for certain. An estimated three hundred US soldiers were killed in action. US Army records did take firmer numbers of those who died of disease, noting that 1,145 perished from diseases like smallpox and cholera.

Despite the high costs the US government bore, the Seminoles were never fully forced out of Florida. Sam Jones (Abiaka) declared, "In Florida, I was born. In Florida, I will die. In Florida, my bones will bleach." Although many Seminoles marched westward, there are still Seminoles who live on reservations in Fort Lauderdale, Tampa, and Immokalee.

By the time Tayor was elected president in 1848, the Gold Rush was on, and thousands of would-be miners were cutting a bloody path westward. In a few years, California became flooded with people, and legalized acts of violence were taking place against the Native Americans there.

William Tecumseh Sherman

Another military officer who played a part in the Trail of Tear epoch was William Tecumseh Sherman, the general who used scorched-earth tactics (where everything is destroyed so no one can use the resources there) against the citizens of Georgia in the Civil War. He cut a path of destruction to Savannah and murdered men, women, children, crops, and animals.

Sherman was born in Ohio in 1820. A decade or so before, Shawnee Chief Tecumseh forged an alliance or confederacy of Native Americans in Ohio. Sherman's father was so impressed with the warrior Tecumseh that he named his son after him. His father defended the name given to his son by critics who wanted to know why a boy should be named after a "savage." Sherman's father replied that in his eyes, "Tecumseh was a great warrior."[76]

In all probability, that is likely where his son got his warrior spirit and the idea of using scorched-earth tactics, which Sherman used against the Confederate States of America and the Plains Indians when he tried to drive them out of Mississippi. Sherman put it bluntly to the Plains Indians: "You cannot stop the locomotive any more than you can stop the sun or the moon, and you must submit."[77]

---

[76] Andrews, Evans. "9 Things You May Not Know About Willian Tecumseh Sherman." *History* (2019). https://www.history.com/news/9-things-you-may-not-know-about-william-tecumseh-sherman.

[77] Ibid.

His orders were to make room for the Transcontinental Railroad by moving the Native Americans west, but in the process, he decided to slaughter their food source. Sherman killed five million buffalo to starve the Native Americans into submission, ultimately forcing them onto reservations.

In *The Real Lincoln*, we are told that General Ulysses S. Grant ordered Sherman, the commander of the US Army in 1865, to "conduct a campaign of ethnic genocide against the Plains Indians to make way for the government-subsidized railroads." In 1866, Sherman wrote to Grant, saying, "We are not going to let a few thieving, ragged Indians check and stop the progress of the railroads." In summarizing Sherman's attitude toward Native Americans, DiLorenzo quotes Sherman. When telling his troops what to do when attacking Native American villages, Sherman said they should "not pause to distinguish between male and female, or even discriminate as to age. If resistance is made, death must be meted out."[78]

Sherman and General Philip Sheridan, the Union General who used scorched-earth tactics in the Shenandoah Valley and said the famous phrase, "The only good Indians I ever saw were dead," committed acts of murder and property destruction under the direction of Abraham Lincoln. Before the Civil War, Sherman fought in the Second Seminole War. Although Sherman expressed remorse for pushing the Seminoles out of Florida, his views were similar to many others in the country. He saw the Native Americans as inferior and standing in the way of progress.

In summing up this chapter, it seems appropriate to quote DiLorenzo about what was happening behind the scenes while violence against Native Americans was being carried out:

"Both the Southern Confederates and the Indians stood in the way of the Whig/Republican dream of a North American economic empire with a subsidized transcontinental railroad, a nationalized banking system, and protectionist tariffs. Consequently, both groups were conquered and subjugated by the most violent means."

---

[78] DiLorenzo, Thomas. *The Real Lincoln: A New Look at Abraham Lincoln*. Crown Forum, 2003.

He also notes the irony that hundreds of ex-slaves called "Buffalo Soldiers" fought with the army against the Native Americans, "inflicting upon another colored race the ultimate inhumanity: violent death or a concentration camp existence on reservations." Here, we can see the story behind the story that is often not told in history books.[79]

---

[79] Ibid.

Chapter 11: Native American Removal: A Timeline

With all the tumultuous events that took place after the birth of America, the tragedy that befell the Native Americans between the 17th and 19th centuries, culminating with the Trail of Tears, is indeed an important epoch in American history. We asked ourselves at the beginning of our historical journey the question of whether Native American displacement was inevitable, and as we examined the events that took place, one should be able to come to their own conclusions.

The various tribes, particularly the Five Civilized Tribes, were slowly becoming acculturated, in effect adapting to European culture. Most of the tribes switched from hunting to agriculture and became prosperous farmers and traders. Others became Christians, and others became officers in the US Army and were honored for their efforts. Our goal here is not to state whether assimilation was a good or bad thing; rather, we are pointing out that most of the Five Civilized Tribes changed to fit in with American society.

But despite this, the settlers pushed westward, with the US military forging a path of destruction that decimated the Native Americans. Again, we cannot help but note the element of greed within the human soul; the speculators were greedy for lands, the railroad barons were eager for profits, and the gold diggers were hungry for the riches in the soil of Native American territory. Even the US government and the idea of Manifest Destiny can be seen as greedy and hungry for more, more, more, whether that was land, resources, or something else entirely.

So, before we conclude this book, let us refresh our memories with a brief timeline of the major treaties that were signed with Native Americans before and shortly after the Trail of Tears. This list is by no means comprehensive; it is meant to be a short guide to help you retain the information you have read while introducing other treaties that didn't quite fit into the framework of the topic.

One of the reasons we can't delve into all of the treaties is the sheer number of them. From 1778 to 1871, the indigenous people across North America signed around 370 treaties with the US, each of them "based on the fundamental idea that each tribe was an independent nation, with their own right to self-determination and self-rule."[80] But as we have noted several times in the text, westward expansion by white settlers led to violations of most of these treaties. They continued to encroach on Native American lands, fraudulent land speculators granted lands to various tribes that already occupied them, and railroad companies demanded land to transport people and goods west.

Here is a condensed history of the treaties the Native Americans signed:

- Treaty with the Delawares or Treaty of Fort Pitt (1778)

  The first formal peace treaty between the US and Native Americans was the Treaty of Fort Pitt. It was signed by the Lenape (Delaware). It was broken in 1872 when the Pennsylvania militia murdered one hundred Lenape and forced the tribe into Ohio Territory.

- Treaty of Fort Stanwix (1784)

  This treaty gave the US sovereignty over all the Iroquois Confederacy's lands as punishment for their support of the British in the Revolutionary War. The Iroquois Confederacy was divided on signing the treaty and was eventually forced to relocate out of parts of New York and Pennsylvania.

---

[80] Pruitt, Sarah. "Broken Treaties with Native American Tribes: Timeline." https://www.history.com/news/native-american-broken-treaties.

- Treaty of Hopewell (1785-1786)

Three treaties were signed by General Andrew Pickins and the Cherokee, Choctaw, and Chickasaw, offering friendship and protection after the War of 1812. They were violated by the encroachment of settlers in the following years.

- Treaty of Canandaigua or the Pickering Treaty (1794)

The Haudenosaunee (Six Nations), consisting of the Mohawk, Cayuga, Onondaga, Seneca, Oneida, and Tuscarora, signed this treaty with the US government. The treaty gave back a million acres that had been taken in the Treaty of Fort Stanwix, but the treaty was later revoked.

- Treaty of Greenville (1795)

The Shawnee, Delaware, Miami, and other tribes banded together to fight the settlers. General "Mad" Anthony Wayne was sent to quell the disturbance and defeated the tribes in the Battle of Fallen Timbers. The Native Americans were forced to cede large tracts of what is now Ohio, Michigan, Illinois, and Wisconsin.

- Treaty with the Sioux (1805)

General Zebulon Pike made an unauthorized treaty with the Dakota leaders, exchanging 100,000 acres for $200,000 to build forts and railroads. Only two of seven tribal leaders signed. Instead of leaving the $200,000 that he had valued the land at, Pike left them with $200 in gifts.

- Treaty of Fort Wayne (1809)

The Delaware, Miami, Eel River, and Potawatomi tribes ceded 2.5 million acres in Michigan, Ohio, Indiana, and Illinois for two cents an acre. Territorial governor William Henry Harrison later broke the treaty and began attacking the tribes in the Ohio Valley.

- Treaty of Ghent (1814)

The Treaty of Ghent was between the US and Britain and ended the War of 1812.

- Treaty of Doak's Stand (1820)

This treaty was said to be a friendship treaty between the Choctaw and the US government. However, Andrew Jackson used threats to get the Choctaw to sign, hinting that the Choctaws would be annihilated if they refused. The Choctaw agreed to give up one-half of their lands in exchange for land in Arkansas and annuity payments.

- Second Treaty of Indian Springs (1825)

William McIntosh signed this treaty with the US government, agreeing to cede all Creek lands east of the Chattahoochee River. The treaty stipulated that the Creeks would move west of the Mississippi.

- Indian Removal Act (1830)

Native Americans were promised land west of the Mississippi if they vacated lands in the southern United States. The act broke treaties that were already in place, with the US and state governments resorted to using military force, trickery, or fraud to get the Native Americans to move westward.

- Treaty of Dancing Rabbit Creek (1830)

The Treaty of Dancing Rabbit Creek was the last major land cession treaty signed by the Choctaw. It was the first Native American removal treaty after the passage of the Indian Removal Act. The Choctaw gave up eleven million acres in Mississippi in exchange for fifteen million acres of land in Oklahoma.

- Treaty of Moultrie Creek (1832)

This treaty established a reservation for several Seminole tribes in the center of the Florida Peninsula if they agreed to cede all other land claims and capture and return fugitive slaves.

- Treaty of Payne's Landing (1832)

This treaty was negotiated by James Gadsen and called for the Seminoles in Central Florida to move west of the Mississippi. Although the treaty was signed by several prominent chiefs, most were coerced into signing. The

Seminoles continued to resist, leading to the Second Seminole War.

- Treaty of New Echota (1835)

A small group of Cherokee signed this treaty, agreeing to move west of the Mississippi for five million dollars. Most Cherokees claimed the treaty was a fraud, but Congress ratified it in 1836. The US government used it as grounds to remove the Cherokee. The Cherokee were forced to march thousands of miles to Arkansas and beyond, with around four thousand dying along the way.

- Treaty with the Potawatomi (1836)

This treaty guaranteed the Potawatomi safety on their reservations in Indiana, but they were soon forced to sell the land for fourteen thousand dollars and pushed westward. Forty of them died along the way.

- Fort Laramie Treaty (1851)

This treaty defined the territory of the Great Sioux Nation of the Dakota and the Lakota (Teton Sioux), who lived in North Dakota, South Dakota, Montana, Nebraska, and Wyoming. The US government did not claim any part of their land. Instead, they sought protection for settlers traveling the Oregon Trail and permission to build roads and forts.

- Treaty of Traverse des Sioux and Mendota (1851)

Fearing for their safety due to encroaching settlers, the Dakota and Mendota ceded millions of acres in exchange for reservations and $1,665,000, which equals about seven cents per acre. They didn't receive either; instead, the money was given to traders to pay debts, and the reservation offer was revoked by the US Senate.

- Treaty of Washington (1855)

The Ojibwe were forced to cede their remaining lands for two reservations on which they were allotted private property. Through this treaty, the US government hoped to destroy the tribal communal laws related to land. The Ojibwe were also forced to become farmers but were still allowed to follow their traditions of hunting, fishing, and gathering.

- Medicine Lodge Treaty (1867)

Following the Civil War, the leaders of the Plains tribes met with the US government to negotiate a treaty that protected their people from violence from the settlers. There were two reservations, one for the Comanches and Kiowas and another for the Cheyenne and Arapahos, but the tribes never signed the treaty. Congress ratified it and then cut down the size of the reservations, withheld payments, and prevented hunting.

- Treaty of Fort Laramie (1868)

This treaty established the Great Sioux Reservation (now called Standing Rock Reservation) for the Dakota, Lakota, and Nakota Nations, along with the Arapaho. It protected the Black Hills and comprised all of South Dakota west of the Missouri River. The treaty was violated in 1874 when gold was discovered in the Black Hills, after which white settlers were given miners' rights. Disputes continue to this day over the Dakota Access Pipeline, which is built on the Standing Rock Reservation.

Although there are many other treaties and events that could be included in this timeline, it still gives us a clear view of the United States' drive to expand westward via the idea of Manifest Destiny. By studying this timeline, we can see how the Native Americans stood in the path of what is called progress today. On the other side, we can also see how often the US government violated treaties to better itself and the settlers who were looking for more land.

If we were to elaborate on all of the treaties the US government violated with the indigenous people of North America and the resulting violence that came with that act, we would need at least one more book, if not more. With this brief timeline, we can ponder the facts laid out by John Bowes in his scholarly essay, "American Indian Removal Beyond the Indian Removal Act," which gives us insight into the broader picture of the removal of Native Americans from their ancestral lands. He makes the point that concentrating on the discourse of the 1830 Indian Removal Act, "which is layered in the language of constitutional authority, civilization versus savagery, property rights, states' rights, tribal sovereignty, and government jurisdiction," leads historians to ignore the broader picture of the removal of Native Americans from the East Coast and the Ohio Valley.[81]

For example, he talks about the Delaware, who were forced to cede parts of New York and Pennsylvania, and the Pottawatomi, who were forced out of the Ohio Valley by French, Dutch, and English colonists. On a broader spectrum, Bowes argues that the historiography of Native American removal is centered around "imperium [empire-building] during the Jackson age" and ignores the fact that Americans were "determined to expand geographically and economically" while "imposing an alien will upon subject peoples and demanding their resources." In other words, the tragic story of the Native Americans should not be limited to just the Trail of Tears or those tribes living in the southeastern United States.

Comparable to the plight of the Cherokee, the "Delaware Trail of Tears" was in many ways worse. Not only were they forced to march from their homes, but they also fled in fear of the military violence that was going on around them, such as the Seven Years' War and the War of 1812. The suffering of the Delaware and Cherokee were instigated by white citizens and bolstered by state governments with the implied approval of the federal government.

The Delaware were pushed westward and southward in rapid motion as treaties were violated in accord with the constant influx of settlers. They were forced to march after they marked treaties with an X, which Bowes quotes Richard Lyons as saying that the X was "a sign of consent in a context of coercion."[82]

The Delaware were expelled from the East Coast toward the Ohio Valley. By the 1790s, six hundred Delaware lived between Saint Louis and New Madrid, both of which are in Missouri. They were then forced to escape to Spanish territory in Texas and Mexico. When Mexico declared its independence, the settlers of

---

[81] Bowes, John P. "American Indian Removal beyond the Removal Act." *Native American and Indigenous Studies*, vol. 1, no. 1, 2014, pp. 65–87. *JSTOR*, https://doi.org/10.5749/natiindistudj.1.1.0065.

[82] Ibid.

Texas committed acts of violence against the newly arrived Delaware, who settled along the banks of the Red River in northern Mexico. The Delaware had no permanent home, and the settlers saw them as being in the way.

After the Treaty of Greenville in 1795, the Delaware were forced to move again, traveling four hundred miles by canoe to the White River in the Wabash River drainage, passing their destroyed villages along the way. And yet again, they were pushed out when white settlers flooded the Ohio Valley and the banks of the Mississippi River after the Revolutionary War. By 1822, the remaining 2,500 Delaware living in Southwest missions were given three years to relocate, ultimately ending up with the Cherokee and Shawnee tribes in Arkansas, where they came into conflict with the Osage.

When the flooding in the Ozarks destroyed their cornfields, and the hunting grounds did not provide enough food, the Delaware began to realize they had been lied to. Delaware Chief Kikthawenund (also known as William Anderson) sadly expressed thoughts that could apply to the nightmare experienced by all of the Native Americans: "The white man now claims our country and demands that we should leave it. And now we know not what to do!"[83]

The idea that the US government perpetrated genocide on Native Americans is a controversial argument today. The term genocide is relatively new, having only been in existence since 1944. Yet, just because the term is new doesn't mean that societies in the past didn't willingly seek to exterminate others because of perceived differences. Our goal here is not to take one side or the other; rather, we want you to be able to come to a conclusion yourself while laying out the arguments historians have.

Some scholars say the US government did not seek to exterminate the Native Americans, with many dying of diseases and conflicts that weren't always started with large-scale deaths in mind. Some conflicts started because the Native Americans had committed a massacre or were planning to engage in war.

However, other historians do believe that what happened was tantamount to genocide, and Bowes is one of them. Some of these

---

[83] Ibid.

historians argue that genocide happens when colonization and expansion take place since one group is almost always pushed to the side. It would have been somewhat easy for US politicians to ignore the plight of the Native Americans as long as they pleased the citizens of the country who voted them into power (the Native Americans would not become citizens of the US until 1924). The forced march of the Five Civilized Tribes saw thousands of deaths, many of which likely could have been prevented, although, with such a long journey and the number of people traveling, deaths would have been inevitable.

And even if one concedes that the settlers did not willingly look to exterminate Native Americans, historians point to the cultural genocide that took place. The Five Civilized Tribes is an excellent example of this, as they abandoned many of their traditional ways to assimilate with Anglo-American culture. The missionary schools that popped up across the country also sought to instill Christianity and the English language in children, forcing them to abandon their traditional language, clothing, and much else.

Regardless of what one thinks of the genocide argument, almost everyone can agree that the Trail of Tears was a tragic epoch in US history.

Conclusion

Chief Joseph, who became chief of the Wallowa band of Nez Perce in the 1870s, offers a quote that speaks volumes. "I believe much trouble and blood would be saved if we opened our hearts more."

Once most of the treaties with the indigenous people had been broken and their court battles defeated or ignored, there was no stopping the push west by the forces of economic growth. Advocates of Manifest Destiny were determined to crush anything or anyone in the way of progress. This clash of civilizations involved endless arguments over sovereignty and states' rights.

Looking at the plight of the beleaguered Native Americans, we can see that the idea of Manifest Destiny was an uncontrollable force leading to either the removal of the Native Americans to government-controlled reservations or their extinction. Yet, we can't help but ask again, was the Trail of Tears inevitable? Could the deaths and suffering of so many Native Americans be avoided? These are questions that are difficult to ask, and you might not have answers for them right now. But we encourage you to read more about this time in history to come to your own conclusions.

Afterword

We don't hear much today about Native Americans today unless it is a story about a protest erupting over a pipeline being built on a reservation, a fight over hunting rights, or hearing the controversy over a sports team using Native Americans as a mascot or a movie where they are portrayed as savages. Native Americans have the highest poverty rate among minorities, despite the casinos they are permitted to build.

The challenges facing Native Americans today include crime, education, voting rights, mental and physical health, environmental problems related to climate change, and the possible extinction of their languages.

Over five hundred tribes that are presently regulated by the government suffer "spiritual and physical violence, societal discrimination, and ... are degraded when they are stereotyped in the media."[84] Since the Great Depression, the Native Americans have not been able to share in the economic prosperity experienced by most of the American population. Around 33 percent of Native Americans live in poverty. Since the 2010 census, the poverty level among the tribes has increased to 49 percent, and as a result, 700,000 or one-third of Native Americans on reservations live in

---

[84] "Native American Issues Today: Current Problems & Struggles 2022." http://www.powwows.com/issues-and-problems-facing-native-americans-today.

poverty.[85]

Some of the issues they currently face are listed below:
- Lack of emergency care and hospitals;
- Multigenerational housing, which can more rapidly spread diseases to other members of the family;
- Job losses due to the recent pandemic;
- Many tribal elders dying off in 2020, leading to the loss of knowledge, language, and connections to history;
- Violence against women and children; 40 percent of women report rape, stalking, or domestic violence;
- Many reservations have a murder rate ten times the national average;
- A 1990 Justice Department report showed 80 percent of physical abuse and rape of Native American women being carried out by non-native people;
- Numerous reported cases of missing and murdered indigenous women.

In regard to the climate crisis, many reservations have valuable resources that are being exploited, including gas, oil, and timber, with some reservations containing gold deposits. Native Americans have stated this exploitation is causing environmental damage to their lands. As a result, many Native Americans are joining social justice and environmental groups to protest fossil fuels, mining, and the installation of pipelines near reservations.

Other notable problems are high school dropout rates, low college attendance, and high rates of obesity, HIV/AIDS, and diabetes. The Indian Health Service (IHS) is underfunded, and the suicide rate for Native Americans between the ages of ten and thirty-four was extremely high in 2019.

Native Americans face issues voting, as there is a lack of polling places. The need to travel long distances to cast a vote is hampered by the lack of transportation. Reservations do not use traditional street addresses, which means their IDs are not always recognized by outside authorities, but with the passing of the Native American

---

[85] Ibid.

Voting Rights Act in 2021, some of these issues have been addressed.

There are only 150 to 170 surviving Native American languages, but they are in danger of disappearing. It has been predicted that by 2050, there will only be twenty Native American languages left. It was hoped that the International Decade of the World's Indigenous People proclaimed by the United Nations would bring attention to these problems.

In "Native American Life Today," Dr. Maria Yellow Horse Braveheart, a Hunkpapa, Oglala Lakota, professor at the University of Mexico, has developed a theory of "historical unresolved grief," or "a psychological wounding ... following the loss of lives, land, and vital aspects of culture." She talks about five hundred years of trauma due to persecution, relocation, and "variations of physical, mental, emotional, and spiritual violence by European emigrants who chose to expand across the continent, in effect decimating the lives of Native American men, women, and children."[86]

According to Yellow Horse, the scars run much deeper, especially since the discrimination continues today. This "collective group trauma," as she calls it, is "passed down on the cellular level," leading to a greater chance of children experiencing increased levels of stress and the potential to develop mental and physical diseases.

One other aspect we will touch on is the struggle for Native American property rights, a battle that is continuing today. There are 6.7 million Native Americans living in the US, with only 22 percent living on reservations under a "federal trust." The rest live in different parts of the country. A federal trust means the federal government assumes all responsibility for the management of the lands. The government essentially acts as the legal owner or trustee through the treaties made between the tribes and the federal government. Federal trusts interfere with property rights and economic opportunities, which negatively impact life on the reservations.[87]

---

[86] "Native American Life Today: Understanding the Destruction." https://pages.nativehope.com/native-americans-today#chp1.
[87] Ibid.

There is a salient quote from *The Atlantic*, an American magazine. Naomi Schafer Riley writes, "Indians have long suffered from what the Nobel Prize-winning economist Hernando de Soto has called 'dead capital.' They may possess a certain amount of land on paper, but they can't put it to use by selling it, buying more to take advantage of scale, or borrowing against it."[88]

Thus, from a historical perspective, we can see that while much has changed for the Native Americans, there is still a lot of progress to be made. They do not have access to the wealth contained in their ancestral lands, and the lack of progress and economic activity has led to continued problems on the reservations where many of them live. By being aware of current events and reading more about historical subjects like the Trail of Tears, people can realize what needs to be done to make sure that everyone lives up to their full potential.

---

[88] Ibid.

Here's another book by
Enthralling History that you might like

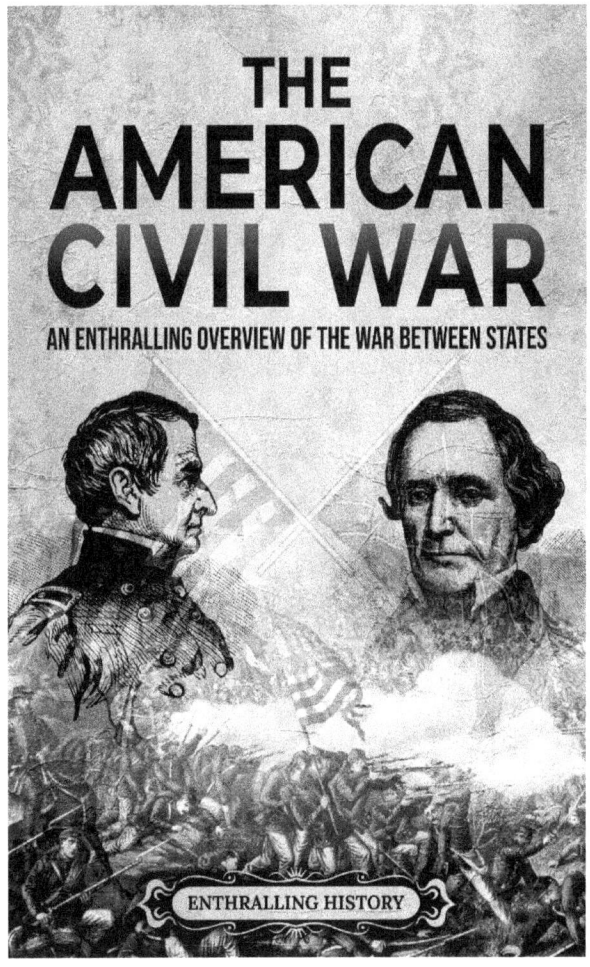

Free limited time bonus

Stop for a moment. We have a free bonus set up for you. The problem is this: we forget 90% of everything that we read after 7 days. Crazy fact, right? Here's the solution: we've created a printable, 1-page pdf summary for this book that you're reading now. All you have to do to get your free pdf summary is to go to the following website: **https://livetolearn.lpages.co/enthrallinghistory/**

Once you do, it will be intuitive. Enjoy, and thank you!

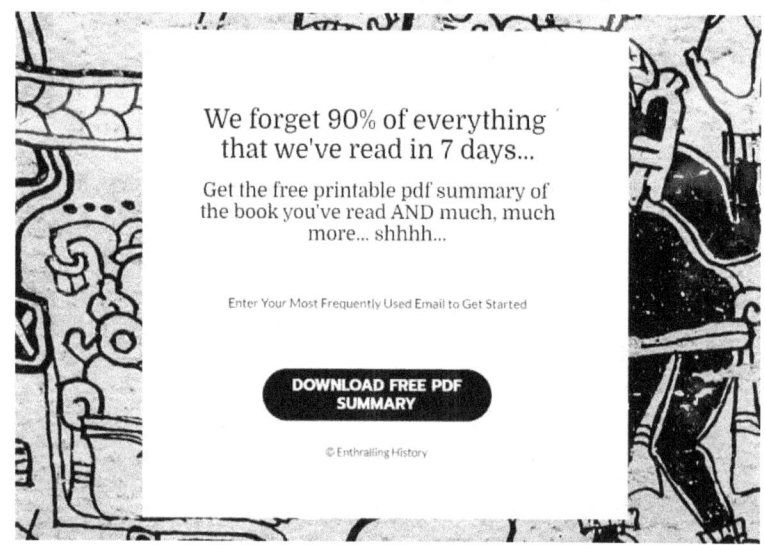

Bibliography

"Abiaka (Seminole Indian Sam Jones) - One of the Greatest Medicine Men in History." https://worldprophesy.blogspot.com/2015/01/abiaka-one-of-greatest-medicine-men-seminole.html.

African American Registry (AAREG), "Billy Bowlegs, Seminole Chief." https://osceolahistory.org/billy-bowlegs-iii-ahead-of-his-time/.

"Andrew Jackson Leaves Office: Martin Van Buren Becomes President." (2014). *Voice of America Multimedia Site.* https://learningenglish.voanews.com/a/andrew-jackson-van-buren/1775693.html.

Andrews, Evans. "9 Things You May Not Know About Willian Tecumseh Sherman." *History* (2019). https://www.history.com/news/9-things-you-may-not-know-about-william-tecumseh-sherman.

Britannica, The Editors of Encyclopedia. "John Ross." *Encyclopedia Britannica*, 28 Jul. 2022, https://www.britannica.com/biography/John-Ross-chief-of-Cherokee-Nation. Accessed 8 September 2022.

Biography.com Editors. "Andrew Jackson Biography." *A&E Networks.* (2017). https://www.biography.com/us-president/andrew-jackson .

Boulware, Tyler. "Cherokee Indians." *New Georgia Encyclopedia*, 20 January 2009, https://www.georgiaencyclopedia.org/articles/history-archaeology/cherokee-indians/ .

Bowes, John P. "American Indian Removal beyond the Removal Act." *Native American and Indigenous Studies*, vol. 1, no. 1, 2014, pp. 65–87. *JSTOR*, https://doi.org/10.5749/natiindistudj.1.1.0065 .

Braund, Kathryn. "Menawa." http://encyclopediaofalabama.org/article/h-3594.

"Broken US-Indigenous Treaties: A Timeline."
https://stacker.com/stories/23887/broken-us-indigenous-treaties-timeline.

Bullman, James A. "William, McIntosh Creek Indian (Muskogean)."
https://www.unknownscottishhistory.com/pdf/William_McIntosh_Creek_Indian_(Muskogean).pdf.

Calloway, Colin. "George Washington Lived in an Indian World, but His Biographies Have Erased Native People."
https://longreads.com/2018/11/07/george-washington-lived-in-an-indian-world-but-his-biographies-have-erased-native-people.

Carlson, Leonard A., and Mark A. Roberts. "Indian Lands, Squatterism, and Slavery: Economic Interests and the Passage of the Indian Removal Act of 1830." *Explorations in Economic History* 43.3 (2006): 486-504. Web. www.sciencedirect.com.ezproxy.liberty.edu.

Casebeer, Kenneth M. "Subaltern Voices in the Trail of Tears: Cognition and Resistance of the Cherokee Nation to Removal in Building American Empire." *University of Miami School of Law.*
https://repository.law.miami.edu/umrsjlr/vol4/iss1/2/.

Cave, Alfred A. "Abuse of Power: Andrew Jackson and the Indian Removal Act of 1830." *The Historian*, vol. 65, no. 6, 2003, pp. 1330-53. *JSTOR*, http://www.jstor.org/stable/24452618.

"Cherokee Nation v. Georgia."
https://en.wikipedia.org/wiki/Cherokee_Nation_v._Georgia.

"Chickasaw Tribe: Facts, Clothes, Food and History."
https://www.warpaths2peacepipes.com/indian-tribes/chickaswa-tribe.htm.

"Chief Dragging Canoe." Video.
https://www.youtube.com/watch?v=vrSXzeIXU5M.

"Collision of Worlds."
https://www.semtribe.com/stof/history/CollisionofWorlds.

Davis, Ethan. "An Administrative Trail of Tears: Indian Removal." *The American Journal of Legal History*, vol. 50, no. 1, 2008, pp. 49-100. *JSTOR*, http://www.jstor.org/stable/25664483.

"Davy Crockett on the Removal of the Cherokees, 1834."
https://www.gilderlehrman.org/history-resources/spotlight-primary-source/davy-crockett-removal-cherokees-1834.

DeRosier, Arthur H. "Andrew Jackson and the Negotiations for the Removal of the Choctaw Indians." *The Historian*, vol. 29, no. 3 (1967).
https://www.jstor.org/stable/24442605.

DiLorenzo, Thomas. *The Real Lincoln: A New Look at Abraham Lincoln.* Crown Forum, 2003.

"Early Choctaw History." https://www.nps.gov/natr/learn/historyculture/choctaw.htm.

Feller, Daniel. *The Public Lands in Jacksonian Politics*. Madison: University of Wisconsin Press.

Freeling, William. "John Tyler: The American Franchise." https://millercenter.org/president/tyler/the-american-franchise.

"General Jesup." http://johnhorse.com/trail/02/c/01.htm.

Genovese, Michael A. & Landry, Alysa. *US Presidents and the Destruction of the Native American Nations (The Evolving American Presidency)*. Palgrave Macmillian, 2021.

Getchell, Michelle. "Indian Removal." Khan Academy. https://www.khanacademy.org/humanities/us-history/the-early-republic/age-of-jackson/a/indian-removal.

Grose, B. Donald. "Edwin Forrest, 'Metamora,' and the Indian Removal Act of 1830." *Theatre Journal*, vol. 37, no. 2, 1985, pp. 181-91. *JSTOR*, https://doi.org/10.2307/3207064.

Haveman, Christopher. "Creek Indian Removal." http://encyclopediaofalabama.org/article/h-2013.

Henig, Gerald S. "The Jacksonian Attitude Toward Abolitionism in the 1830s." *Tennessee Historical Quarterly*, vol. 28, no. 1, 1969, pp. 42-56. *JSTOR*, http://www.jstor.org/stable/42623057.

Hershberger, Mary. "Mobilizing Women, Anticipating Abolition: The Struggle against Indian Removal in the 1830s." *The Journal of American History*, vol. 86, no. 1, 1999, pp. 15-40. *JSTOR*, https://www.jstor.org/stable/2567405. Accessed 7 Oct. 2022.

Hickman, Kennedy. "American Revolution: Major General Anthony Wayne." ThoughtCo, Aug. 28, 2020, https://thoughtco.com/major-general-anthony-wayne-2360619.

Higginbotham, William. "Trail of Tears, Death Toll Myths Dispelled." *The Oklahoman*, 1988. https://www.oklahoman.com/story/news/1988/02/28/trail-of-tears-death-toll-myths-dispelled/62660437007/.

"History: Chickasaw Nation." https://www.chickasaw.net/our-nation/history.aspx.

Hryniewicki, Richard J. "The Creek Treaty of Washington, 1826." *The Georgia Historical Quarterly*, vol. 48, no. 4, 1964, pp. 425-41. *JSTOR*, http://www.jstor.org/stable/40578419. Accessed 14 Oct. 2022.

"Introduction." https://www.semtribe.com/stof/history/introduction.

Jefferson, Thomas. *Notes on the State of Virginia*. University of North Carolina, 1982 (originally published in 1785). https://www.jstor.org/stable/10.5149/9780807899809_jefferson.

Johansen, Bruce. "Jacksonian Indian Policy, 1818–1832." https://americanindian2-abc-clio-com.ezproxy.liberty.edu/Search/Display/2219984.

"John Ross: Principal Chief of the Cherokee People." https://tnmuseum.org/junior-curators/posts/john-ross-principal-chief-of-the-cherokee-people.

"Jumper, John (ca. 1820–1896)." The Encyclopedia of Oklahoma History and Culture. https://www.okhistory.org/publications/enc/entry?entry=JU002.

Keating, Jessica. "The Assimilation, Removal, and Elimination of American Indians." *The McGraph Institute for Church Life*, (2020). https://mcgrath.nd.edu/assets/390540/expert_guide_on_the_assimilation_removal_and_elimination_of_native_americans.pdf

Kennedy, Roger. "Jefferson and the Indians." *The University of Chicago Press, Vol. 27, No. 2/3*. (1992). https://www.jstor.org/stable/1181368.

Kievit, Joyce Ann. "Treaty of Dancing Rabbit Creek." *The American Mosaic: The American Indian Experience*. https://americanindian2-abc-clio-com.ezproxy.liberty.edu/Search/Display/1670319.

Knox, Henry. "To George Washington from Henry Knox." https://founders.archives.gov/documents/Washington/05-04-02-0353.

Landry, Alysa. "Martin Van Buren: The Force Behind the Trail of Tears." (2018). *ICT. An Independent Nonprofit News Enterprise*. https://indiancountrytoday.com/archive/martin-van-buren-the-force-behind-the-trail-of-tears.

Little, Becky. "How Boarding Schools Tried to 'Kill the Indian' Through Assimilation." *History* (2018): Web. https://www.history.com/news/how-boarding-schools-tried-to-kill-the-indian-through-assimilation.

Littlefield, Daniel F. "Cherokee Removal." *The American Mosaic: The American Indian Experience*. https://americanindian2-abc-clio-com.ezproxy.liberty.edu/Search/Display/1595705.

Marszalek, John F. "Sherman, William Tecumseh (1820-1891)." *Encyclopedia of the Great Plains, (2011)* University of Nebraska. http://plainshumanities.unl.edu/encyclopedia/doc/egp.war.043.

"May 28, 1830 CE: Indian Removal Act." https://education.nationalgeographic.org/resource/indian-removal-act.

McIver, Stuart. "Bring Me the Head of Osceola." *Sun Sentinel.* https://www.sun-sentinel.com/news/fl-xpm-1988-01-31-8801070155-story.html.

"Memorial of the Cherokee, 1829." http://recordsofrights.org/records/39/memorial-of-the-cherokee.

"Native American History Timeline." https://www.history.com/topics/native-american-history/native-american-timeline.

"Native American Issues Today: Current Problems & Struggles 2022." http://www.powwows.com/issues-and-problems-facing-native-americans-today.

"Native American Life Today: Understanding the Destruction." https://pages.nativehope.com/native-americans-today#chp1.

"Native Americans." https://www.mountvernon.org/george-washington/native-americans/.

Niderost, Eric. "A Massacre of U.S. Soldiers Started the Second Seminole War." *Warfare History Network*, (2022) Vol. 22, No. 3. https://warfarehistorynetwork.com/article/a-massacre-of-u-s-soldiers-started-the-second-seminole-war/ .

Pauls, Elizabeth Prine. "Trail of Tears" Encyclopedia Britannica, 28 Mar. 2022, https://www.britannica.com/event/Trail-of-Tears. Accessed 24 August 2022.

Petrini, Andrea R. "The Enlightenment of Thomas Jefferson." https://elonuniversity.contentdm.oclc.org/digital/collection/p15446coll2/id/11/.

Pruitt, Sarah. "Broken Treaties with Native American Tribes: Timeline." https://www.history.com/news/native-american-broken-treaties.

Pulley, Angela. "Elias Boudinot." *New Georgia Encyclopedia*, 03 September 2002, https://www.georgiaencyclopedia.org/articles/history-archaeology/elias-boudinot-ca-1804-1839/.

"Report of Henry Knox on the Northwestern Indians." https://pages.uoregon.edu/mjdennis/courses/hist469_Knox.htm.

"Seminole History." https://dos.myflorida.com/florida-facts/florida-history/seminole-history/.

"The Creek War of 1836 in Alabama, Georgia, and Florida." https://exploresouthernhistory.com/secondcreekwar.html.

"The Muscogee (Creek) Nation – Legends of America." https://www.legendsofamerica.com/na-creek/.

"The Seminole Wars." https://www.seminolenationmuseum.org/history/seminole-nation/the-seminole-wars/.

"The Trail of Tears: They Knew It Was Wrong." Video. https://youtu.be/qalhDKLrWEQ.

"Third Seminole War." https://www.u-s-history.com/pages/h1156.html.

"Trail of Tears: Creek Dissolution." (2002). https://www.liquisearch.com/trail_of_tears/creek_dissolution.

Warren, Michael. "Dade's Massacre Reenacts Start of Second Seminole War." https://floridatraveler.com/dades-massacre-recalls-seminole-history/.

Watts, Jennifer. "John Ross: Principal Chief of the Cherokee People." https://tnmuseum.org/junior-curators/posts/john-ross-principal-chief-of-the-cherokee-people?locale=en_us.

"Westward Expansion (1807-1912): Land Policy and Speculation." https://www.sparknotes.com/history/american/westwardexpansion/section2/

www.ingramcontent.com/pod-product-compliance
Lightning Source LLC
Chambersburg PA
CBHW070339010526
44107CB00004B/554